Playboy's
Illustrated Treasury
of
Gambling

A Ridge Press Book ☀ Crown Publishers, Inc. New York

Playboy's Illustrated Treasury of Gambling

by David Carroll

Technical consultant: Darwin Ortiz

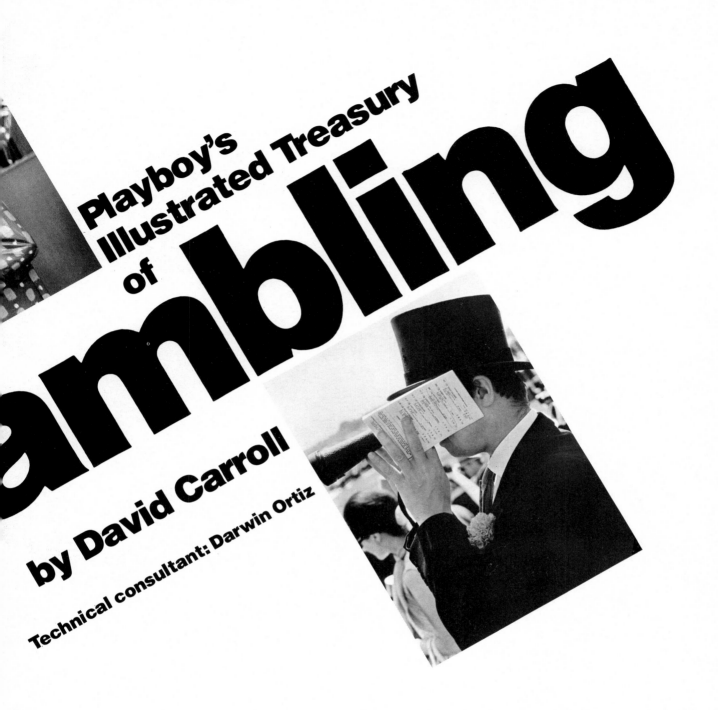

Editor-in-Chief: Jerry Mason
Editor: Adolph Suehsdorf
Project Art Director: Harry Brocke
Associate Editor: Ronne Peltzman
Associate Editor: Joan Fisher
Art Associate: Nancy Mack
Art Production: Doris Mullane
Picture Research: Marion Geisinger

Library of Congress Cataloging in Publication Data

Carroll, David, 1942-
  Playboy's illustrated treasury of gambling.

  "A Ridge Press book."
  1. Gambling. I. Title.
GV1301.C34   795'.01   77-6629
ISBN 0-517-53050-3

Printed and bound in Italy by Mondadori Editore, Verona.

Contents

Introduction page 14

1

Where the Action Is
page 18

2

Cards and Card Games
page 48

5

The Horses
page 146

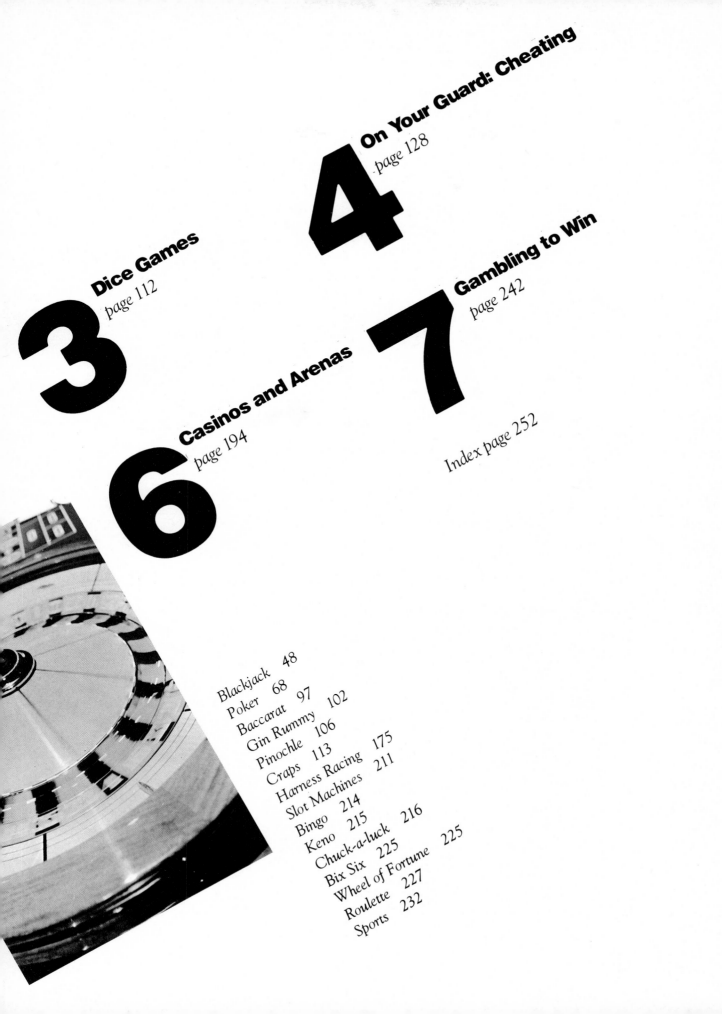

3 Dice Games
page 112

4 On Your Guard: Cheating
page 128

6 Casinos and Arenas
page 194

7 Gambling to Win
page 242

Index page 252

Blackjack 48
Poker 68
Baccarat 97
Gin Rummy 102
Pinochle 106
Craps 113
Harness Racing 175
Slot Machines 211
Bingo 214
Keno 215
Chuck-a-luck 216
Bix Six 225
Wheel of Fortune 225
Roulette 227
Sports 232

Introduction

Life is a gamble. The odds against making it to a womb in the first place are staggering. Once there, the chances of emerging are scarcely 100 percent. The fourscore years that follow are a continuing contest against fate's shifting odds, played with the disconcerting knowledge that the house must win in the end. Lose, say the iron rules of probability. Man must lose whether he sport at a game of life or a game of chance. And lose over the long run he almost invariably does. What is most interesting about it all is that forearmed with knowledge of his own fate, man continues to gamble at both life and games with undiminished vigor, as if it is not the outcome that ultimately matters but the spirit of the play.

Man is thus a gambling animal, the only one we know. He gambles everywhere. Always. It may not be on a lottery ticket or a horse race. The mountain climber risks his life with each Himalayan ascent, the speculator his cash on every new investment. In this book, however, we are interested in a specific sort of gambling. It is the staking of something valuable, with consciousness of risk and hope of gain, on the outcome of a game of chance.

If this book has fallen into your hands by choice you must be interested in gambling. If you're interested in gambling, chances are you've gambled once or twice. And if you've gambled . . . well, you know it can be a complicated affair.

But why? I don't mean why is it complicated—we'll get on to that later. But why do you—and I—and he and she, why do we all like to risk our precious dollars on the random spin of luck's wheel?

There are, of course, the deep, dark reasons, the secret innermind provocations, the sexual insinuations of poker bids, the Oedipal overtones of twenty-one. We'll get to these, too. But for now let's investigate the less sticky motivations.

Like, for instance, the fact that everybody likes to get something for nothing (and corollary to this statement, which explains why we so often retire losers, that "you can't get something for nothing"). This is as good a reason as any, especially for those of us from the push-button society. Press a button, the toast pops. Press a button, the car window drops. It's the split-second world, a perfect environment for the practice of gambling—for the psyche of the bettor is based on the promise of instant results. What a man can make in his entire life at his job he can hypothetically earn in an hour at the roulette wheel. Gambling is the perfect occupation and preoccupation of the impatient.

Then, again, it's exciting. Life on the whole, one must admit, is often a slow affair. There are the highs and the spins, yes, but these aren't as common as the shampoo commercials would have us believe. As a rule, it's the daily pace, nine-to-five ennui. Somehow the spaces must be filled. Some of us do it by racing fast cars, others by solving chess problems. And some gamble. We gamble because it's fun, because it produces the kind of electric thrill we once felt long ago, the first time we stole a candy bar from the dimestore. It's a kick, intoxicating, romantic, dangerous, exhilarating, exhausting, fearsome, abandoned, despairing, and euphoric all rolled into one—not many experiences offer such a broad spectrum of emotions.

There's another reason, obvious but important: winning. We like to win. We like kewpie dolls and door prizes. And, even more, we like money. When all is said and done, gambling is about money. But here is the big question: will we ultimately come out ahead if we gamble? The odds say no. To gamble over the long term is to lose. Nonetheless the gambler is undaunted. Because, being basically a mystic, he believes that the cold steel of statistics affects only the other guy. For the real believer there's a big kiss from Lady Luck just around the corner, a secret gift of luck headed his way amid the slings and arrows of outrageous randomness. The genie of wheel and dice whispers to the gambler that he, he, HE alone is special, that he alone is above the laws of chance that bind all others. Did he win the last time out? You see, that proves it! Did he lose? Never fear. Tomorrow his luck will change.

Like an abiding pleasure, gambling has a thousand faces, some sensitive, some appalling. It brings out the best, it brings out the worst. It is an outlet for ambition, aggression, and dreams, an instructor in probabilities, prudence, and silence. It tests us, amuses us, and sometimes breaks us. It teaches many useful things, if we care to listen, things concerning the private and sometimes very surprising facts of our own very human weaknesses and strengths. In the final analysis, gambling is all about ourselves.

1. Where the Action Is

"Yesterday's crimes," a discerning Roman wrote, "are to-day's fashions." Nowhere has this proven more true than in gambling. Once thought of as both a crime against God and a crime against society, gambling is today the coming thing. Nevada's decades-long monopoly on legal casino gambling has been broken by a plebiscite in Atlantic City. Once one of America's favorite playgrounds, the seaside resort had fallen on hard times. Now, with the legalization of gambling, property values have soared and the entire city vibrates with an excitement born of the conviction that the best is yet to come. Nor is it likely that Atlantic City and Las Vegas will be able to carve up all the action between them. New York State, perpetually on the verge of bankruptcy, is eyeing the massive revenues that casino gambling promises and insiders claim that legalization is a sure-thing bet. Florida, New Mexico, Arizona, and other states are also considering taking the plunge. But if Las Vegas is worried it's not letting it show. New hotel-casinos continue to go up and old ones continue to undergo expansions. The theory seems to be that if America is developing gambling fever, everyone is going to benefit.

Meanwhile, more and more states are adopting other forms of gambling. Connecticut's recent decision to allow jai-alai has produced profits beyond even its supporters' wildest expectations. That kind of success is not likely to be ignored by other revenue-hungry states. There is legislation presently pending in thirty-seven states to legalize a wide variety of gambling ventures, including lotteries, bingo, off-track betting, dog racing, cardrooms, and policy betting.

Nor are state and local governments the only financially hard-pressed organizations who are turning to gambling as a painless tax on their constituents. New York City has adopted legislation permitting "Las Vegas Nite"—gambling sponsored by charitable organizations. In an earlier era such legislation would have met insurmountable opposition by church groups. However, these same religious organizations became among the strongest supporters of the bill, apparently concluding that if people are going to insist on enjoying themselves in spite of sermons to the contrary, some good may as well come from it. So church-going high rollers need no longer be content with Friday-night bingo. Now they can play blackjack, craps, and chuck-a-luck with clear consciences under church auspices.

Looking around in any gambling casino, race track, off-track betting parlor, or private poker game it doesn't seem as if the nation's gamblers really feel the need for any moral justification. Despite inflation and recession, America is continuing its evolution into a leisure culture. People are taking their pleasure more seriously. And that's bound to mean more gambling. While the traditional gambling games continue to grow in popularity, new games like jai-alai and baccarat have been imported from Europe and ancient games like backgammon are being rediscovered and given a new lease on life.

An American Muse

Gambling has a long, if not always honorable, tradition in America. It was a popular pastime in colonial times with lotteries being a particular favorite. However, the event that ushered in the great age of American gambling was the purchase of the Louisiana territory. New Orleans was host to the first real casino in America, opened in 1827 by a slick Caribbean islander named John Davis. Accustomed to shabby backrooms, Southern odds-makers had never seen its likes. Here was a real European-style casino—ornate, elegant, with carpeted halls and murals in the foyer, a free buffet, the best wines and cigars, mahogany tables for faro, roulette, vingt-et-un, and private rooms for brag, écarté, and a game later known as poker. But that wasn't all. Davis was an innovator. Rather than charge a fee at the door or levy a tax on winnings, he devised a novel scheme for milking his patrons. He mathematically rigged the odds of every game to favor the house. The house eventually had to win—a simple notion that revolutionized the trade. For the casino, the gamble was now out of gambling.

From New Orleans, gamblers fountained outward in two directions. Some moved to the East Coast where the action was always heavy, while others traveled up the Mississippi. The latter group availed themselves of the mode of transportation called the riverboat. By 1835 there were two hundred and fifty of these pleasure machines on the Mississippi and Ohio rivers. Within their confines, riders luxuriated in sumptuous cabins or toasted their journey in ballrooms hung with gilt mirrors and crystal chandeliers.

The fact that these vessels traveled at an average speed of four miles per hour meant that passengers had plenty of time on their hands and were always in search of amusement. There to satisfy them was the ever-present riverboat gambler. Dressed in Parisian leather boots, broadcloth jacket that hung to the knees, slouch hat, charcoal gray trousers, frilled blouses ornamented with diamond buttons, and with cane in hand, the riverboat gambler was no more conspicuous on deck than, say, the paddle wheel. Fifteen hundred of these rascals worked the steamboat route from New Orleans to Louisville, with the majority of them concentrated on the river below St. Louis, where their favorite prey—rich plantation owners and cotton magnates—were found in abundance. The games they played included whist, boston, vingt-et-un, faro, and such venerable swindles as three-card monte and the shell game. In addition, the riverboat gambler helped popularize a hitherto neglected game: draw poker.

Many of the gamblers spawned in the South moved on to join the steady current westward. In 1849 this current turned into a tide with the cry of GOLD! Mining camps and gold towns sprang up, each with its own saloon and gambling hall. In Brodie, California, a reporter boasted that there were forty-seven saloons, ten faro tables, twenty-three dance halls, six retail shops, and one hotel.

Gold was everywhere; money was everywhere. It was the age of the instant city. Towns appeared from nowhere, the largest and most sudden being San Francisco. It was here that the lucky striker came to wager his gold in gambling houses like the famous Eldorado Hotel. Here tables for faro, vingt-et-un, and chuck-a-luck extended to the horizon. Drinks were served at an inflation price of seven dollars a shot, but the entertainment was free, featuring the best in minstrel music and Irish tenors. What's more, most of the croupiers in San Francisco were female, exiles from Paris. The French government, eager to clear the Champs Elysées of streetwalkers, had shipped over boatloads of these *belles dames*.

But in Frisco gambling came before carnal pleasures. "Gambling was *the* amusement, the grand occupation of many classes," wrote an observer in 1850. "Around the tables themselves the players often stood in lines three or four deep, everyone vying with his neighbor for the privilege of reaching the board, and staking his money as fast as the wheel and ball could be rolled or the card turned."

The flavor of these Western gambling spots was strictly backwoods and uncouth, a contrast to the plush

East Coast gambling palaces where there was no smell of rawhide or whiskey-breath. The Gold Coasters were here, eager to spend the millions they had hustled from the poor. There to accommodate them was John Morrissey, an ex-world-champion prize fighter. He was one of the first to realize that the more elegant a casino appears, the more its clientele will feel obliged to spend.

Morrissey selected a brownstone in lower New York and in 1862 opened it in style. The result pleased even the most demanding millionaires, including Jim Fisk and many of the Vanderbilt clan. What made this club so attractive was not just the rosewood interiors.

First of all, it was exclusive and private, two characteristics that appealed to everyone's sense of importance. Secondly, the newly arrived guest, having once passed the butler-bouncer at the door, was left alone, at liberty to wander freely through the libraries, the velvet sitting rooms, the music chambers and private apartments, or to enjoy possibly the finest cuisine in New York City without ever once being "guided" to the gambling room. In any case, most of the guests came to gamble, and did.

Morrissey's club was an immediate success and resulted in dozens of imitators. Soon all the big cities along the East Coast had their rich man's gaming salons. In the

latter part of the 1800s gambling became the chief amusement of the rich, and membership in a private gambling club was an emblem of prestige. But a new century brought a new world. No sooner had the 1900s dawned than reformers launched massive antigambling campaigns. In 1901 the licenses of dozens of gambling houses were revoked. The following year, the clubs were closed permanently. The era of posh, private gaming salons in America was over. The sport of gambling, however, did not cease. Since then, gambling houses continue to operate illegally, generally with protection from local authorities.

A Free Lunch

Legalized casino gambling did not return to the United States until the Nevada legislature voted it back in 1931. This monumental event in gambling history did not attract much notice at the time. For years thereafter Las Vegas remained a sleepy little desert town with a few saloons featuring gambling. All of this began to change when mobster Bugsy Siegel built the Flamingo Hotel, the first of the super-resorts on the Strip. Even then most of the players came from the West Coast. As little as twenty years ago there was no direct air service from New York to Las Vegas. Since many of the biggest gam-

*Twenty-four-hour action for those
fascinated by the roll of the dice, the
spin of the wheel, the turn of a card. After
a rigorous game of craps, casino patron can
move on to more relaxing keno or wheel
of fortune (opposite top and bottom).*

blers in the country were on the East Coast, something had to be done to get them out there. That something was the junket.

High rollers have always received "comps" (complimentary room and board) in the major Las Vegas hotels but the junket concept expanded the practice to a mass scale. Here again, the Flamingo was a leader. The first junkets to Las Vegas were sponsored by the Flamingo and organized by a man named Bernie Cohen; soon afterwards, Julie Weintraub, the best-known and most successful of the junket agents, began performing the same service for the Dunes Hotel. Today, junkets from major cities across the country are sponsored by most of the major Las Vegas casinos as well as casinos in the Bahamas, Puerto Rico, Europe, and soon possibly Panama. In Britain, however, the government frowns on such activities.

A person going on a junket receives free transportation on a charter flight plus what the casinos call RFB (room, food, and beverages) privileges. In other words, all expenses are paid. The really big bettors also receive VIP treatment everywhere they go, including ringside seats at the best shows and just about anything else they ask for. In return, all the junket goer has to do is gamble. It sounds like the player is getting away with highway robbery. He isn't—not anymore, anyway.

In the late sixties when the junket business was first getting started, big abuses were common. Many people went out, gambled very little or not at all, and enjoyed a wonderful vacation at the hotel's expense. In some cases the scams were more elaborate with hotels being defrauded out of large sums, sometimes by sophisticated con artists working in teams.

Today, junket organizers have become considerably more professional. Anyone out for a free ride should

OTB *windows at Grand Central
Station in New York are busy, as bettors
choose their horses—determined by everything
from skilled handicapping to a good guess.
Right: Computers add, sort, and transmit
bet totals and payoff odds to tote boards.*

27

be forewarned. A first-time junket goer is often required to put up as much as five thousand dollars in front money. When he reaches the hotel this money is returned to him in the form of casino chips. In addition, the better junket agents also put applicants through thorough credit checks. Finally, some will only consider applicants who have been recommended by regular junket goers in good standing. Not many freeloaders can come up with thousands of dollars in cash, establish a credit line of five or ten thousand dollars, and provide references to boot.

Of course, once there, no one can force you to gamble. But they can make sure that you never go on another junket if you don't. All junket goers are carefully watched and rated, depending on the amount of time they spend gambling, the size of their bets, and the speed with which they pay off their markers. This rating deter-

mines whether you will be asked to join the next junket, be asked along only if there are empty seats on the plane, or not be allowed back under any circumstances. Your rating also determines how you are treated if you are allowed on a subsequent junket. This may range anywhere from the complete VIP route to barely civil treatment. Junket goers are definitely not created equal as far as the casino is concerned. There is a strict caste system based not on race, creed, or color, but on the amount of action you give the house.

Still, if you are the right kind of player, a junket to a major casino can be an unforgettable experience. And the picture can only improve from the player's standpoint. As more states legalize gambling, the junket will, no doubt, become one of the major weapons the casinos will use in competing for customers. If Las Vegas wants those legendary big Eastern gamblers to bypass nearby Atlantic City and bring their business to Nevada, they will have to make the trip as enjoyable and inexpensive as possible. At the same time, the Atlantic City clubs are not likely to sit by idly and watch their clientele being shipped wholesale across the country by the Vegas junket organizers. It might become a buyer's (gambler's) market with junket "wars" proliferating.

The Poker Capital of the World

Since poker is thought of as the great American pastime, considered by foreigners to be the quintessential American game, it is ironic that playing poker is illegal in most of the fifty states. Of course, it is only illegal if you bet money, but as any poker player will tell you, poker isn't poker without money. Although a few states are considering legalizing poker cardrooms, poker is perhaps the least exploited source of government revenue from gambling. The folly of this oversight is dramatically illustrated by the case of Gardena, California, a small community twelve miles from downtown Los Angeles. It hosts six legal poker cardrooms: the Eldorado, the Gardena, the Horseshoe, the Monterey, the Normandie, and the Rainbow. These clubs are open twenty-four hours a day, six days a week. Each club closes on a different day of the week so that a poker addict can always find action.

Poker was legalized in Gardena in 1936. Draw poker was considered not to constitute gambling because it is a game of skill—a verdict with which any poker player will agree, at least when he is winning. Surprisingly, stud poker, a game requiring greater skill, was classified as a game of chance. Today it is the one form of poker that is illegal to play in Gardena.

All the clubs offer versions of draw poker and lowball and some also have high-low. The clubs have no house dealers so the players take turns dealing, as in a private game. In fact, the only thing to remind you that you are not playing in a private game is the young lady who comes over every half-hour to collect the house's fee. This fee ranges from one to five dollars, depending on the size limit of the game you are playing. This fee is the only charge for playing and gives the player a better break than the Las Vegas practice of cutting each pot.

As in Vegas, all the clubs hire house players. Their only purpose in doing so is to help fill empty seats to keep a game going. In Las Vegas, shills are officially called "game starters." Although this term isn't used in Gardena it aptly describes their function. These players are on their own as far as winning or losing. So if you discover such a house player, don't jump to the conclusion that the club is engaged in some dark conspiracy to defraud you.

Unlike Las Vegas, Gardena does not have games with really high stakes. There are many one- and two-dollar games, and the highest legal bet in any game is twenty dollars. There are some professional poker players who frequent these cardrooms, but most of the players are retired persons who play daily or working people who play several evenings a week to relax, the way some people frequent the corner tavern. But don't let that make you overconfident if you find yourself in a game with them. The frequency with which they play together along with their familiarity of the rapid style of play usually followed in these clubs makes many of the regulars stiff competition for an outsider.

The chances for passage of some of the pending bills to legalize poker in other states seems good, particularly because of the fact that the Gardena clubs earned over $15 million in 1976. In the meanwhile, we can all take comfort in the fact that poker is safe in at least one

*Money on a dream. Lucky
number brings joy and up to
$1,000 a week for life to
winners of state lotteries—
to others the hope that
next time it will be them.*

community in the country. When a bill was introduced
in 1958 to outlaw poker in Gardena, it was defeated by a
vote of three to one. It's nice to know that someone is
guarding the flame.

Take a Number

At the moment, the frontrunner in the trend toward legalized gambling in this country is the lottery. More
states have adopted lotteries than any other form of gambling, and more of the legalized gambling bills pending
throughout the nation concern lotteries than any other
kind of wager. This is in the best American tradition.
There were legal lotteries in each of the thirteen colonies, and George Washington, Benjamin Franklin, and
John Hancock were among the men who sponsored
them. Thomas Jefferson was in the process of organizing
one when he died. Such illustrious institutions as Har-
vard, Princeton, and Yale were largely financed through
lotteries. To date, every state that has adopted a lottery
has enjoyed good results with it. However, none has
even begun to approach the success of the biggest lottery
of all time: the numbers game.

From its modest beginnings in Harlem in the
1920s this illegal numbers racket has grown to become
the largest and most popular lottery in the world, out-
grossing the combined totals of all legal lotteries
throughout the United States and Europe. In New York
City alone the estimated daily handle is over one million
dollars a day.

One reason for its success is the fact that it offers
more action than any other lottery. There is a new winning three-digit number selected each day. Players may
bet a number "straight" or in "combination." A straight
bet wins only if the player's three-digit number comes up
in the order he specified. The payoff is 400 for 1 (or

sometimes 300 for 1) minus a 10 percent commission for the runner. A combination bet (also known as a box bet) pays off if the selected three digits come up, regardless of the order. The player has a much better chance to win, of course, but collects less on his bet if he does win. In addition, most policy banks also accept single-number bets. Thus, if you sneezed three times this morning, the mystical significance of this event might lead you to bet that the third digit in today's winning number will be three.

Through the years different methods have been used to determine the winning number in an effort to find a process that can't be rigged. The present method is to take three digits from the parimutuel payoffs of certain races at some predetermined major racetrack. The exact details of computation and the racetrack used differ from city to city since the numbers racket is not controlled by a single national organization. Rather, there are a large number of policy banks throughout the country, often several in a single city. That means that the winning number in Detroit on a given day is not likely to be the same as the winning number in Brooklyn.

The selection of a different number each day is an important part of the appeal of the numbers game. For people who play the numbers, the game often plays a significant role in their lives. Predominantly poor and working class, they turn to the numbers for a source of escapist entertainment. Dreaming of what they will do with their winnings, contriving new methods to compute their "lucky number" for the day, puzzling out the numerological significance of their dreams, waiting with anticipation throughout the day as each new winning digit is announced—the numbers game is the "Let's Make a Deal!" of the poor. A weekly or monthly lottery just can't provide that much fun.

Another feature that most state lotteries don't provide is a player's right to choose what number he will bet on. In most legal lotteries you are stuck with what they hand you. What difference does it make? Mathematically, none; psychologically, it makes all the difference in the world. A gambler wants to feel that he has some control over his own fate. Intellectually, every intelligent crap player knows that he has just as much chance of winning with another player throwing the dice as he does on his own roll. But the next time you are in a casino, notice how many players increase their bets when they are handling the dice. In your heart of hearts you know that a randomly selected number just can't have as much chance of hitting as the first three digits of your young daughter's birthday. Particularly when you are planning to use the winnings to buy her a birthday present—after you have donated 20 percent to the church as you promised Saint Francis in your prayers last night if he would make your number come up. The numbers racket grosses more than $10 billion a year because it understands human nature.

It is not surprising that state and local governments should want to get in on this bonanza by adopting new lotteries more closely patterned after the numbers game. But there are barriers. One is the fact that much of the money presently taken in on the numbers is already going to government, particularly law enforcement. No major policy bank in a big city can exist without protection. The politicians that have a good thing going for them through their connections with organized crime are not likely to give it up without a fight. This is, of course, another good reason for legalization. Gambling is the number-one corrupter of police and is sure to remain so until the temptation is removed.

This is not to imply that all politicians who op-

Text continued on page 41

Games of chance are played in every echelon of society.
Top r and l: Since the eighteenth century, Italians
have played lotto, a game similar to bingo.
Above: Monte Carlo has traditionally been the rendezvous
of royalty and celebrities, but now they have discovered other
locations, such as the casino in Deauville, France (r).

34

Anything-goes gambling is
aided and abetted by gaudy settings
(r), intriguing machinery and
equipment. These Nevada sites offer
amusing slots (below and bottom r),
21 and roulette tables (bottom l, this
page and opposite), dice and chips, and
hypnotically spinning roulette wheel.

pose a government-run numbers operation do so out of venal motives. The numbers banks in poor urban areas are big local employers. The runners and agents are all ghetto dwellers. Therefore, most of the numbers money collected in the ghetto stays in the ghetto. This would probably change under a state-run operation. Thus, politicians representing these areas often oppose legalization of a numbers operation out of a desire to protect their constituents' interests.

Many other people oppose a legal numbers game out of what they deem to be humanitarian reasons. Such a program would earn revenues from those least able to pay and would thus constitute a regressive tax. The reality is, of course, that people are already paying such a tax—to the Mafia. Sociological and humanitarian arguments of this kind are often a mask for the patronizing belief that the poor don't have a right to the vices the rest of us enjoy. One thing can be said in favor of the numbers game over other forms of gambling: no one has ever gone broke playing it. Many middle class and even wealthy people have hopped a plane to Las Vegas and met complete financial ruin at the dice or roulette tables. This has probably never happened to any numbers player in the history of the game simply because most bet only a dollar or two each day and some as little as fifty cents or even a quarter. In other words, for the average player the numbers habit costs about as much as the smoking habit. But cigarettes don't pay off at 500 to 1 and playing the numbers won't give you cancer.

In the end, the determining argument will probably be financial. States need the money. Connecticut, Maryland, Massachussetts, New Jersey, and Rhode Island have already adopted daily lotteries and the most successful have been those patterned most closely after the numbers game. More are sure to follow.

The Best is Yet to Come

What we are dealing with here is a kind of domino theory. When New Hampshire instituted the first state lottery of modern times in 1963 there was wide criticism from many quarters. But within a decade, a dozen other states had joined in. In gambling, as in everything else, nothing succeeds like success. As Americans become more mobile, states find themselves fighting for revenue not only from their own residents but also from out-of-staters. To an extent, they are all competing for the same buck. If Atlantic City succeeds in its dream of becoming Las Vegas East, other states are not likely to sit by while their tourist dollars are siphoned off by New Jersey. Atlantic City could easily start a casino-gambling trend much like the one New Hampshire started in the lottery field.

Of course, fiscal concerns are only a part of the picture. Americans are becoming more pleasure-oriented and more and more people are becoming convinced that government has no right legislating private morals, gambling included. Many law-enforcement officials are making it known that they want out of the gambling sphere. They are disturbed by the police corruption generated by illegal gambling and they are becoming convinced that the only way to fight organized crime in this area is to compete with it. Finally, they believe, as do a great many Americans, that the police have more pressing business to attend to. Thus, we have today a unique convergence of cultural, political, and fiscal factors that could well usher in a gambling renaissance.

"Casting lots," Proverbs says, "causes contentions to cease," and Thomas Jefferson praised legalized gambling as "a salutary instrument wherein the tax is laid on the willing only." You can't argue with God and country.

Glossary of Gambling

Gamblers have always been famous for their lingo, especially since many of their phrases have become an accepted part of English speech. Words and terms like *crestfallen* (from the fallen cockscomb of a rooster defeated in the pit), *underhanded* (an allusion to crap shooters who place their hands under the table), *playing both ends against the middle* (to bet on both contestants in a prize fight), a *double-crosser* (the prizefighter who loses "crosses up" those who have bet on him), *aboveboard* (a card player who keeps his hands above the board, i.e., the table, shows he's not cheating), *to get one's goat* (when race horse trainers kept a pet goat near a horse's stall to calm it down before a race, the goat was sometimes stolen by rival horsemen to make the horse even more nervous than before) all have their roots in the gambling past. Following is a list of some of the better-known and widely used terms from the gambler's vocabulary. How some of these words came into being is quite obvious; others, well, it's just about anybody's guess.

Terms

Action. *Betting. Fast play between gamblers. The chance to gamble.*

Ante. *Money put into the pot before the deal.*

Bait. *A game in which the odds are so ridiculously stacked that only the greenest player would participate. Bait also pertains to the sucker. The sucker is the "bait" of the hustler; also, when the hustler "baits" the sucker he allows him to win several times before moving in for the big kill.*

Bank. *The house, the casino itself, or any player who sets the odds and controls the game. Sometimes "bank" also refers to the dealer in a casino game.*

Behind the sink. *Broke. Cleaned out.*

Betting interval. *The period of time between bets when each player is given the right to drop out of the game.*

Bluff. *To bet on a poor hand in the hopes that others, seeing the bluffer betting so liberally, will think he has a strong hand and drop out of the game. Mostly used in poker.*

Board. *The table on which a gambling game is played.*

Bobbed. *Cheated. Swindled.*

Bones. *Slang for dice.*

Break the bank. *To exhaust the revenues of the house, a misnomer. No one really takes the house for all its money. They simply win so much at a single table that the house must close that table down for the night.*

Buck the tiger. *To play faro.*

Burn a card. *In blackjack, to bury a card face-up on the bottom of the deck.*

Bust. *To lose a hand and/or all one's money.*

Cane. *The croupier's stick, usually made of hickory, rattan, or bamboo, with which the dice are retrieved after each roll.*

Card sense. *An intuitive wisdom and feeling for card games.*

Carpet joint. *A plush, high-class casino. The opposite of a sawdust joint (q.v.).*

Clean move. *A well-executed cheating manipulation.*

Cold. *Unlucky. Unable to win. Riding a streak of bad luck.*

Cold deck. *A stacked deck, one in which the cards have been previously arranged.*

Cooler. *The same as a cold deck.*

Crimp. *To bend the cards in a certain way, usually at the corners, so they can later be identified in different positions around the playing table.*

Crosslift. *A cheating technique used at poker in which two or more players conspire through their combined betting to force other players out of the pot or to bet more than they otherwise would have on losing hands.*

Dead card. *A card that is officially out of play.*

Dead-man's hand. *A poker hand showing two aces and two 8s, said to have been the cards held by Wild Bill Hickok the moment he was shot from behind in a saloon.*

Doctors. *Loaded dice.*

Doubling-up. *The practice of doubling a bet after each loss in the hope that eventually a winning number will come up and all losses will be recouped.*

Edge. *The advantage. The house advantage is its "edge."*

Even money. *A bet in which the odds favor neither bettor. Fifty-fifty is an even-money bet.*

Face card. *A jack, queen, or king.*

Fish. *A sucker. An easy mark. A loser.*

Fix. *To influence or arrange the outcome of a game.*

Flat joint. *Carnival lingo for any crooked game such as a rigged wheel of fortune, a fixed bingo match, etc.*

Floating game. *Any gambling game, especially craps, which is constantly being moved from one location to another in order to avoid police detection.*

Fly bet. *An unusual or unlikely bet.*

Fold. *To hand in one's cards. To stop playing.*

Force the cut. *To cause a player to unwittingly cut the deck at a predetermined spot by previously secretly bending certain cards at the spot. This creates an air-pocket in the deck to which the unsuspecting player usually cuts. The technique is used by card cheats to nullify the effect of an honest cut.*

Gaffed. *Gimmicked. Crooked gambling equipment is said to be gaffed.*

The handle. *The amount of money wagered in a gambling house or at a specific table over a given period of time. The total amount bet on a race or a day's racing.*

Head-to-head. *A one-to-one game situation.*

Hedge a bet. *To cover one bet with a compensating bet in order to prevent total loss or to insure breaking even.*

Hot. *Lucky. Winning continuously.*

House. *The casino; also, the people who operate a game.*

House limit. *The highest bet allowed by a particular casino or particular game.*

House percentage. *The percentage held back on winnings by the house to ensure profits.*

Index. *The number and suit emblem printed on the corner of a card, such as the 10 and spade sign on the 10 of spades.*

In the black. *Lucky. Winning continuously.*

In the red. *Unlucky. Showing consistent losses.*

Joint. *A casino or gambling house.*

Kitty. *A pool to which all players contribute and from which winnings and royalties are paid.*

Lay odds. *To bet a larger amount of money against a smaller amount of money.*

Layout. *A diagram, complete with compartmentalized designs, betting zones, and information on the odds, laid out on the table of a casino game.*

Levels. *Honest dice or cards.*

Loads. *Loaded or crooked dice.*

Loose table. *A table in a casino at which only a few patrons are gambling.*

Make good. *To add enough to the pot to match the previous bets. Also, to pay up one's gambling debts.*

Mark. *A sucker.*

Memphis dominoes. *Slang for dice.*

Misdeal. *A crooked or wrongly executed deal.*

Misses (or missouts). *Crooked dice that prevent the player from making his point.*

Moniker. *The house emblem usually found marked on the casino's dice or chips.*

Nickel game. *A gambling game that pays the correct odds. Also, a small-time game.*

No-limit game. *A game in which the players can bet as much money as they wish.*

Nut. *The operating expenses that must be met by a gambler or gambling operation before they can begin to show a profit.*

Odds. *The mathematical possibilities of an event or situation occurring. Specifically in gambling, a ratio like 2 to 1 expressing the amount by which a winning bet will be paid.*

Thus, in craps a ten-dollar bet on number 4 will pay twenty dollars. A horse quoted at 10 to 1 will, if it wins, pay ten dollars for each dollar bet on it.

Office. *A secret sign used for cheating purposes among crooked gamblers.*

Open. *To start the betting in a game.*

Overlay. *Odds better than reasonably justified.*

Over the hump. *A gambler who is ahead of the game and is thus gambling with the house's money.*

Paper. *Marked cards.*

Passers. *Dice that are gimmicked to help the player make his points.*

Penny ante. *A game with low betting limits.*

Pips. *English word for the suit emblems printed on the face of the cards—clubs, spades, hearts, and diamonds.*

Pit. *An area on the floor of a casino closed to the general public that houses the manager and other officials of the casino.*

Pot. *The total amount of money or chips bet in a single round or deal.*

Roping. *Cheating.*

Rough hustle. *An attempt by a dealer to inveigle a large tip from one of the players.*

Sawdust joint. *A low-class gambling establishment. The opposite of a carpet joint (q.v.).*

Second deal. *A crooked deal in which the dealer deals the second card from the top.*

Shiner. *A cheating device, specifically a mirror worn on a ring or held in the palm for reading the cards.*

Shoe. *A box from which the dealer deals the cards.*

Short end. *In a bet, the money put up by a person taking the odds.*

Smart money. *Money intelligently bet; also, money bet by those with inside knowledge of the odds or of some other determining factor.*

Steer joint. *A crooked gambling casino.*

Sure thing. *A bet that has to win.*

Take. *The amount earned by the casino. Also, to "take" or to be "on the take" means to be receiving bribe money.*

Take a bath. *To lose heavily.*

Take the odds. *To accept a bet with the odds against you.*

Tats. *Slang for dice.*

Tony. *A signal word among dice players meaning loaded dice. One player asks another, "Did you bring Tony tonight?"*

Touch. *To ask someone for a loan.*

Unload. *To secretly get rid of unwanted cards from one's hand when cheating.*

Viggorish. *The percentage taken by a casino in any gambling game.*

Zing it. *To shoot the works. To bet all one's money.*

Characters

Alone player. *A gambler who plays by himself and is not associated with any house or syndicate.*

Banker. *The dealer, or anyone who sells chips at a casino. Also, any participant in a game who handles the money.*

Base dealer. *A card cheat who specializes in dealing off the bottom of the deck.*

Bindle-stiff. *A rube. An inexperienced gambler.*

Bookie (or Book). *A person who determines the odds in a horse race or other event and who takes and pays off bets.*

Boxman. *In craps, the employee of the casino who oversees the game.*

Bug. *An inveterate gambler, i.e., one who is bitten by the gambling bug.*

Card mechanic. *A cheater, one skilled in manipulating the cards.*

Chalk bettor. *A horse bettor who always bets on the favorite.*

Check copper. *Someone who steals chips from the gambling table when the croupier (q.v.) is not looking.*

Cool-off man. *The member of a crooked gambling ring or* confidence mob whose job it is to hang around afterward and calm down the mark, hopefully ensuring that he won't go to the police.

Counter. *In blackjack, someone who keeps tabs on each card in play, usually as part of an overall system.*

Cowboy. *A high, wild bettor. An unpredictable player who throws his money around and makes extravagant bets.*

Croupier. *An employee of the casino who runs the games, pays and collects on bets, and occasionally deals.*

Dead-head. *Someone who is not gambling, usually because he has lost all his money.*

Dice detective. *An employee of the casino whose job it is to pick up the dice that have fallen to the floor.*

Dice mechanic. *A cheater, one skilled in the use of dice.*

Dizzy-izzy. *A systems player.*

Easy pigeon. *A sucker.*

Eldest hand. *The player to the left of the dealer.*

Fader. *A dice player who covers the present shooter's bets.*

Fast company. *Knowledgeable gamblers who are hip to playing strategy and the more common cheating techniques.*

Floorman. *The supervisor of a casino.*

Grifter. *A confidence man.*

Heel. *A small-time gambler.*

High roller. *A gambler who risks large sums of money.*

Itemer. *A cheater's confederate, one who signals his partner information on the other players' hands.*

Joe Goss. *The proprietor of a casino (from Australian rhyming slang, "Joe Goss, the boss").*

Jonah. *A superstitious player. Anyone believed to bring bad luck to a player.*

Kibitzer. *Someone who offers constant advice but never plays the game himself.*

Lop ear. *A sucker.*

Mason. *Someone who refuses to gamble.*

Mechanic. *See* Card *and* Dice mechanic.

Nutman. *Someone who finances a game or a casino.*

Outside man. *An employee of the casino who works on the street, persuading passers-by to patronize his particular establishment.*

Peanuts. *A tight-money gambler.*

Pit boss. *An employee of the casino whose job it is to oversee all the action on the floor, to make sure no one cheats or is cheated, and generally to supervise all play.*

Plunger. *A gambler, one who "plunges" into the game without heed of the consequences.*

Posing Dick. *A gambler with a flashy, extravagant style.*

Praying John. *A superstitious gambler who believes that oaths, incantations, etc., will influence the dice.*

Punter. *A gambler.*

Rabbit. *A timid card player who is easily bluffed or talked down.*

Rock. *A tight-fisted gambler, one who will never make a silly bet.*

Roper. *A cheater.*

Runner. *An agent in the numbers game.*

Shill. *An employee of the casino planted conspicuously around the gambling house to entice others to gamble. In a crooked house the shill will be allowed to win, thus inspiring onlookers to try their luck.*

Shooter. *The person rolling the dice.*

Shortstop. *A conservative gambler, one who makes only small bets.*

Steerer. *Same as Outside man (q.v.), someone who hustles business for the casino.*

Steward. *An official at the race track responsible for overseeing all races and protecting against foul play.*

Stiff. *An unlucky gambler (also an unlucky number). Also, in blackjack, any hand with a hard count of 12 to 16.*

Tin. *A policeman or house detective.*

Welsher. *Someone who refuses (or is unable) to pay off a bet.*

2. Cards and Card Games

Cards, those mysterious, ancient, ubiquitous, dangerous, loveable pasteboard decorations. Where they really come from no one knows. How many fortunes they've made, how many lives they've ruined, how much laughter they've evoked over a jolly game—no one can say. There are more than five thousand games people can play with cards plus hundreds of variations, and new games are appearing all the time. Cards are in fact the backbone of the gambling game world.

Do You Know Your Cards?

The inveterate card player prides himself on knowing cards inside and out. This may be true—but only with the games he plays. How about the cards themselves? He's looked at these pretty things from the time he was a child, but does he really know them? The pictures on all modern decks show practically the same design. How many right answers can you give?

1. Which king stabs himself in the head with a sword?
2. How many jacks are seen in profile?
3. Which king doesn't have a mustache?
4. Which is the only king who smiles?
5. How many queens hold flowers?
6. Do any queens hold flowers?
7. Which king looks in profile?
8. Three queens look to the viewer's left. Which queen looks to the right?
9. Which queen has the longest hair?
10. Are all the kings holding swords?
11. Which queen wears a collar with a triangle in it?
12. Which jack has four-leaf clovers on his chest?
13. Which jack has a leaf protruding from his cap?
14. Which king holds a round globe?

Answers: *Look at the cards.*

One right—*Brilliant*	Three right—*Transcendent genius*
Two right—*Downright amazing*	Four right—*You cheat*

A Crash Course in Casino Blackjack

Although blackjack is a relatively new game, it is probably the most widely played banking game in the world today. Where it comes from no one knows, though just about every country in Europe claims to have invented it.

Its popularity is not hard to explain: the game is simple to play, requiring little practice; yet like chess, which can be learned in a night, it takes years to play well.

Basically there are two kinds of blackjack: private and casino. For those who are beginners at the game and wish to try their luck at the nearest casino, the following quickie course is offered with hopes that after reading it you'll know how best to place your bets at the gaming world's favorite sport.

Principles

The cast of characters in casino blackjack includes a house man, who is permanent dealer, one to six players seated around a semicircular layout, and a pit boss, whose on-the-spot arbitration settles all arguments.

The object of the game is deceptively simple. The player tries to obtain a higher card-count than the dealer without exceeding a count of 21 (hence, the alternate name of the game, "twenty-one"). If the player goes over 21 he "busts," or loses, and automatically surrenders his bet regardless of the cards held by the dealer. If his cards total more than the dealer's but less than (or exactly) 21 he wins and receives a payoff.

All bets in blackjack are made against the dealer, never against other players. Bets are always made before the deal, and are placed in an individual betting box located on the layout directly in front of each player. In blackjack it would appear that the player is afforded many advantages. He has a number of betting options that are closed to the dealer; one of the dealer's cards is always on display; and the dealer is bound by the house rule to stand pat at a count of 17 and draw at a count of 16. All these features are seductively appealing to the prospective player, as the first-glance allurements of any casino game are designed to be. But here is the inevitable kicker: when a player busts, the dealer, who always plays last, wins *regardless* of the cards he holds. This means that if every player at the table busts, the dealer does not even have to finish out his hand.

In blackjack the card suits are disregarded. Only the numbers have significance. The 2s through 9s are counted at face value; the 10s, jacks, queens, and kings are each worth 10, and the ace can be counted either as 1 or 11, depending on how the gambler wishes to play it. In general, a gambler always values an ace as 11 until his count goes over 21, in which case it counts as 1. A hand in which there are no aces or in which an ace is counted as 1 is known as a "hard hand." A hand containing an ace counted as 11 is "soft." A "blackjack," the object of the game, comes when an ace and a 10-count card are received in the opening deal. This equals 21, giving the player a blackjack, and, except in the case of a tie with the dealer, an automatic win. However, if in a tie the dealer gets 21 with three or more cards, the player still collects. That is, the dealer can only tie a natural with a natural of his own.

In some casinos, blackjack is played with a single deck, though so many successful counting systems have been launched of late that many houses now employ four (sometimes two, seven, or eight) decks dealt from a card box called a "shoe." When a single deck is used, the cards are shuffled by the dealer and cut by a player. The dealer then "burns" the first card by putting it face-up on the bottom of the deck. When four decks are used, the cards are shuffled and an indicator card is placed somewhere near the end of the deck, face-up, to mark the spot where the cards must be reshuffled.

The betting starts with all wagers placed in the betting box. When all bets are down, the dealer starts his deal clockwise, usually giving two face-down cards to each player and one up and one down to himself. Variations on this deal, incidentally, are found in many casinos.

If the dealer has dealt himself a face-up ace or 10-count card he checks his face-down or "hole" card to see if it makes a blackjack. If it does he automatically wins and collects from all players—unless another player also has a blackjack, in which case there is a "standoff" and no money is exchanged. On the other hand, if one of the players gets a blackjack he turns over his cards and collects from the dealer at 3 to 2 odds. This, by the way, is the only time a blackjack player gets odds at better than even money. The only exception is a rather risky ploy called "insurance," which will shortly be explained.

If no one gets blackjack on the opening deal the player to the dealer's left starts the action. Does he want to "stay," that is, does he decline more cards from the dealer, trusting that the two cards he holds will beat the dealer? Or does he want an additional card, a "hit," in order to increase his point count? What he will do depends on what he is holding.

For example, if the player is holding a 4 and 5, making 9, naturally he will take a hit. He has nothing to lose, for the highest card he could get would still not bring

*Rustic, pine-knotted room
and player piano harks back to
days of Old West, when—as
now—a lively card game with friends or
foes and a drink was often
major source of entertainment.*

him over 21. So he says "hit me," and gets, let's say, a 9, making his total 18. If he's wise he'll stay.

Let's pretend, though, that he's not wise, and he asks for a hit. He gets a jack, counting as 10, which with the 18 brings him way over 21. He has busted and must pay off his bet to the dealer. Suppose, however, that our foolhardy friend has gotten lucky and was dealt a 2 instead. His total would have been 20, a hard hand to beat. He would then have stayed and waited to see if the dealer could beat him.

The dealer meanwhile continues around the table. When everyone has played he plays out his own hand. If his two-card count is 17 or over, the house rules say he must stay. If his count is 16 or below, the rules say he must hit and continue to hit till his count reaches or exceeds 17. If the dealer holds a soft 17, the rules still hold true; he must stay, and this is true for all counts of 17 as well.

When the dealer has finished play, either having busted or received a score below 21, he moves counter-clockwise around the layout paying off those whose score is higher than his own and collecting bets from those he has topped. If both player and dealer have the same hand it is a standoff. When all bets are collected the dealer picks up the cards, puts them in the discard pile, and deals a new round.

This is the basic game of blackjack. But that's not all there is to it. There are the refinements, the so-called "proposition bets." First of these is "pair splitting." This happens when a player dealt two cards of the same number value is given the option of playing out each card as a separate hand. If while playing out these two hands the player then receives still another of the same number card he can split this one too and so on up to a maximum of four splits. Naturally the good player will only want to split the good cards (we will learn about good and bad

splits presently). This gives him a nice percentage advantage over the dealer, plus a chance to bet twice as much money on a good card.

Another proposition bet is "doubling down." The rules for this procedure vary from casino to casino. Some, like those in the lower Caribbean, allow doubling only on 10 and 11. Others, such as the Puerto Rican houses, permit it on 11 only, while still others, like those in Las Vegas, let the player double down on any two cards he wants. Doubling down is done by turning the cards face up after the original deal and announcing that one wishes to double his bet. The dealer then gives the doubler *one* more card, face down. The player must stand pat on these and await his fate.

Finally there is "insurance betting." In many casinos, when the dealer's face-up card shows an ace, the players are allowed to bet an amount equal to half their original bet that the dealer *has* a blackjack. If the dealer does have blackjack he pays off the insurance bet at 2 to 1, the best odds in the game. If not, he collects the bet and play continues as usual. Insurance is thus a form of protection the house offers the player. But beware of Greeks bearing gifts. The price on this protection comes high, as we shall soon see.

The Intelligent Blackjack Player's Strategy

Those who call blackjack "a game of luck" have to be lousy blackjack players. They wouldn't consider making such a statement otherwise. True, the game has its mechanical elements, especially in the house rules that seemingly reduce the dealer to something less than a robot. Yet dealers in Las Vegas and elsewhere make good money, so there must be more to their actions than meets the eye. The secret lies in the fact that they know there is no such thing as a chance move in blackjack, that no play can

Chances of Reaching and Exceeding 21				
	with hard 13	*with hard 14*	*with hard 15*	*with hard 16*
Total chances of busting	27 in 52	29 in 52	30 in 52	32 in 52
Chances of busting with one card	20 in 52	24 in 52	28 in 52	32 in 52
Chances of getting from 17 to 21	25 in 52	23 in 52	22 in 52	20 in 52

Chances of Reaching and Exceeding 21			
	with 2 cards	*with 3 cards*	*with 4 cards*
Odds on making 21	24–1	13–1	19–1
Odds on getting 16 or better	1.5–1	1.9–1	4.3–1
Odds on busting		2–1	1–2

The Hard Hands		
Player Holds	*Dealer Shows*	*How to Play*
2–11	2–ace	hit
12	2,3	hit
12	4–6	stand
12	7–ace	hit
13	2–6	stand
13	7–ace	hit
14	2–6	stand
14	7–ace	hit
15	2–6	stand
15	7–ace	hit
16	2–6	stand
16	7–ace	hit
17	2–ace	stand
18–20	2–ace	stand

The Soft Hands		
Player Holds	*Dealer Shows*	*How to Play*
19	2–ace	stand
18	2–8	stand
18	9, 10	hit
18	ace	stand
17	2–ace	hit

ever be made at random. They know that blackjack savvy consists of both understanding the constantly varying odds and of psyching out the dynamics of play: when not to stand, hit, double down, and split pairs.

There are of course many systems for playing good blackjack, some of them puzzlingly dissimilar. The rules presented here are somewhere between radical and conservative play. They are sound, proven tactics, slightly on the safe side, perhaps, but intelligent. Though no guarantees come with these or any other rules, it is a fact that by following them any player can become a pretty good blackjacker in a pretty short amount of time.

When to Hit, When to Stand

Any blackjack player knows what to do with a pair of kings, or a jack and 10. That's not playing blackjack, that's just being lucky. What about "stiff" hands, those which number between 12 and 16. These are the hands that percentagewise kill the player. Now is when play separates the wise from the foolish. Does one hit or stand? What are your chances of reaching 21? Study or memorize the charts opposite and you will discover some of the answers.

Splitting Pairs

Pair splitting helps whittle down the house's edge. The danger is that the inexperienced player wants to split every pair that comes into his hands, sometimes worsening rather than improving his odds. The decision whether it is best to split or not depends on what your cards are and on the dealer's.

Doubling Down

Here is another nice aid, but, again, the gambler must know *when* to use it. In general the best time to double down is when the dealer shows a weak card, say a deuce

Splitting Pairs	
Card	*Strategy*
ace	Always split aces. NOTE: When splitting aces the casino allows a player to draw *only* one card. Nonetheless the odds are still good enough to make ace splitting pay off.
2,3	Split 2s and 3s when the dealer shows 2 through 7.
4	Split 4s only when the dealer shows a 5.
4–6, 10	Never split these cards.
6	Split 6s when dealer shows 2 through 7.
7	Split 7s when dealer shows 2 through 7.
8	Split all 8s.
9	Split 9s unless dealer shows 7, 10, or ace.

Doubling Down	
Rule One	Always double on an 11. This puts one in strong position to get a "pat" hand (one that counts 17 through 20) without any chance of busting.
Rule Two	Double on 10 if dealer shows a 2 through 9.
Rule Three	When allowed—many casinos bar it—double down on 9 when dealer shows a 2 through 6.

through 6, and when the player has something strong, especially an 11. Remember that the player can draw only *one* card when doubling down.

Insurance

Insurance bets look nice at a 2 to 1 payoff. But unless you have already been clocking the number of 10s in play it is risky business. The reason for this is that there are sixteen 10-count cards in a deck, and thus when the dealer is showing a 10-counter the odds are he will get a blackjack only 16 times in 51, a pretty poor bet. So unless you know approximately how many 10-counters have fallen, leave insurance alone.

Pointers for the Blackjack Player

The beginning blackjack player should be aware of the following four important points. First, a newcomer to blackjack may be likely to play a ridiculously conservative game, each time refusing a hit at 12 or less and thinking that since it is now impossible for him to bust, the odds must be in his favor. Sounds good—until he learns that this little maneuver gives the house a whopping 18 percent edge. Stay away from ultraconservative blackjack. Liberality tempered with common sense and knowledge of the odds is the best approach.

Second, blackjack is the only casino game in which there is head-on play between house and player, which means that a good blackjacker should know all he can about the dealer. This may not be possible on a personal level, of course, although by gambling at the same table for a long time one comes to learn a dealer's weak spots. (Watch him especially a few minutes before he goes off his shift. He's tired. Now's the time he's most likely to make mistakes.) It *is* possible though to learn the style of the house man's play. On each deal pay careful

attention to his cards. They are as important as your own. If it looks as if he will be forced to draw to a bust, play conservatively. If it looks like he may gain a pat hand, play with more abandon. Know the mechanical advantages that the house offers and use them to their fullest. Basically, there are four such advantages:

1. The dealer must stand at 17, hit at 16. This means that if the player holds 18 and the dealer 17, the dealer must stay even though he will automatically lose, an obvious boon to the casino goer.

2. Remember that if wisely made the proposition bet can be the blackjack player's best friend. The best of these, percentagewise, is doubling down.

3. Since the player and not the dealer gets a 3 to 2 payoff on a blackjack, the money balance is kept more even between house and player.

4. The simple fact that the dealer's cards are on display while the player's are not allows the latter to choose his strategy with greater finesse. Each of these advantages can and should be exploited to their fullest by the thoughtful blackjack enthusiast.

Third, to play really excellent blackjack one must learn at least the fundamentals of card casing or counting. For instance, simply by keeping track of all the 10s played throughout a game the expert blackjack player has a good approximate knowledge concerning the odds of himself or the dealer receiving a blackjack. Tens however are just one number that can be cased. There are innumerable methods, many of which work. The best known is enumer-

ated in Edward O. Thorp's book, *Beat the Dealer.* However most of these systems are complicated (Thorp's was figured out on a computer, discussed later in this chapter); and also, many have been emasculated by the new house practice that allows a shuffle after every deal, consequently disrupting the caser's count. Despite these handicaps, however, counting, if done surreptitiously, can still be the best way to shave the odds.

The fourth important point to remember is that the range of skill at blackjack is so wide that the house percentage varies from 18 percent for terrible play to close to a player advantage of 2.3 percent for expert play. The differences can be listed in this way:

Range of Skill for Blackjack Players		
Poor Player (house takes about 18 percent or more)	*Good Player* (about even)	*Expert Player* (player advantage up to 2.3 percent)
Plays randomly, betting wildly and playing hunches.	Plays and bets systematically.	All features of Good Player, plus an ability to remember a majority of cards that have been played.
Does not know the odds.	Knows all the odds.	
Does not understand how or when to make proposition bets.	Follows a proven system of when to hit, stand, etc.	
Poor money management. Chases his bets. Bets conservatively when winning and doubles bets when losing.	Manages money with a purpose. Understands how to ride a winning streak and when to stop completely.	
Poor concentration. Talks when playing or accepts free drinks offered by the house.	Concentrates completely on the game. Is not easily distracted by the dealer or by goings-on in the room. Does not drink while playing.	
	Makes good use of the proposition bets, playing them only when the odds are favorable.	

Playing the Systems Game at Blackjack

A wag once quipped that bringing a betting system to a casino is like trying to use a computer to alter the law of $1 + 1 = 2$.

This is not quite true. A lot depends on luck when you're using a system. Naturally. Gambling always depends on luck. And a lot depends on how much money you have to begin with. And on how good your memory is, how fast you are with figures, how finely honed your common sense is, how well you make decisions. Don't let anyone fool you though, even the best players use systems, even gents like Nick the Greek who scorned them in public but who could remember every card played in a game and who spontaneously evolved systems according to the needs of the moment.

In the preceding pages a simple but effective strategy for the player at blackjack is outlined. This strategy, known among blackjack players as "basic strategy," requires that the player base his decisions on two pieces of information: the total of his hand and the value of the dealer's up-card. However, the player has access to a great deal more information if he knows how to utilize it. Remember, blackjack is not an independent trials process. The previous hands *do* influence the subsequent hands in that once a card has been dealt out it is taken out of play. In other words, if you are dealt a certain card you know that you cannot receive that same card in any subsequent hand until the cards are reshuffled (unless, of course, more than one deck is used).

This knowledge can have significant implications for the skilled player. For example, you have been keeping track of the cards and realize two thirds of the way through the deck that all sixteen 10-count cards have been played. Later, the dealer receives an ace as his up-card and offers you insurance. Naturally, you decline the offer realizing that with the deck completely depleted of 10s the dealer cannot possibly have 21. This is, of course, an extreme example but it illustrates the point that knowing what cards have been played out can put you in a better strategic position.

Similarly, if all four aces are played out early in the game you would be wise to reduce the size of your bets until the cards are reshuffled. No aces means no naturals with their 3 to 2 payoffs and, hence, less chance for the player to come out ahead. Actually, every time any card is removed from play it affects the player's chances of winning, for better or worse. If you were to play blackjack for an extended length of time against a deck that had a single card missing you would win either more or less often than normal just because of the absence of that one card. How much the results differed from the norm and in which direction would depend on the value of the card that was missing. With the aid of a computer it is possible to determine what impact every card in the deck has on the player's chances of winning. Thus, if you had access to a computer while playing you could feed it the value of each card as it was played out and you would always know just how good your chances of winning the next hand were. What is the advantage of that? Simple—every time your chances of winning were better than usual you would increase the size of your bet. Every time they were below average you would cut back on your bet. When you won you would usually be winning big bets; when you lost you would usually be losing small ones.

Since bringing a computer to a casino is considered bad form by most management personnel, a method had to be devised for approximating a computer's calculations. Several methods have been devised, and some of the best are discussed below.

Advanced Counting Strategies. The first man to bring

blackjack counting to public notice was mathematics professor and computer expert Edward O. Thorp. Thorp based his system on the fact that a player's chances of winning at blackjack are proportionate to the ratio of 10-count cards (tens, jacks, queens, and kings) to non-10s in the deck. The larger the percentage of 10s left, the better the player's chances. Thorp's system involves keeping a running count of how many 10s are left in the deck as well as the total number of cards left. Since the cards are usually dealt out and collected pretty rapidly by the dealer, this is not easy. A great deal of private practice is required before a player can pull this off under fire in a casino. Once he has his count, there is still more work to be done. When the time comes to bet, the player must mentally convert the 10s/non-10s ratio into a decimal number. The size of this number determines the size of the bet.

But Thorp went much further. The basic strategy given earlier provides the best hitting-and-standing, splitting, and double-down decisions when one doesn't know the composition of the deck. However, when one knows, for example, the ratio of 10s to non-10s in the deck, much more accurate strategic decisions become possible. With the help of extensive computer calculations, Thorp reduced this strategy to several tables. The "standing table," for example, lists all possible values for the dealer's up-card along the top and all the possible player-hand totals along the left side. The player need only look up the dealer's up-card and follow the column of figures below it until it intersects the row of figures that correlate to the value of the player's hand. There he will find a certain decimal number. If the index of the deck (the decimal number representing the 10s/non-10s ratio) is higher than that number he draws another card. Otherwise he stands.

Blackjack basics. Top l to r: After bets are made, dealer deals two face-down cards to players, one up and one down to himself. If he has ace and 10-count, he wins. Bottom l to r: Pair splitting. Experts say always split aces and 8s, never 5s and 10-counts. When dealer's up card is an ace, player may take "insurance"—not usually a good bet.

*Before each game, dealer
shuffles deck(s), player cuts
deck, dealer completes
cut, then removes top card
and turns it face
up on bottom of deck.*

The only problem is that anyone seen consulting such a chart in a casino is likely to receive an escort to the door, especially if he has been winning all night. The table must be carried around inside the player's head. And there are similar tables for determining when to double down on a hard hand, when to double down on a soft hand, and when to split pairs. They each have to be committed to memory so thoroughly that the necessary strategic decisions can be made with no telltale hesitation that might tip off the casino as to what is actually going on.

When Thorp first tried his system out in Las Vegas he was so successful that the casinos barred him from their premises and instituted rule changes limiting the player's advantages. Fortunately, these rule changes (barring the splitting of aces and restricting double downs) were rescinded when play started dropping off at the tables. The details of Thorp's system are given in his book *Beat the Dealer.* Keep in mind, though, that for success with this system you should practice to the point where you can count through a deck faster than you can recite the alphabet and drill on those tables until you know them better than your own name.

The Thorp system is based on a generalization— the richer the deck is in 10s the better for the player. Other generalizations have led to other systems. For example, the more high cards there are in the deck the better the player's chances, the more low cards the less chance of winning. This observation, backed by computer game simulations, has led to another group of counting systems sometimes known as high-low strategies.

In such a system the low cards (2, 3, 4, 5, 6, and 7) are each given a point value of plus 1. The high cards (9, 10, and ace) are each given a point value of minus 1. Eights are neutral and count as zero. Starting against a full deck the player begins his count at zero. Every time he sees a low card he adds 1; every time he sees a high card he subtracts 1. At any given moment the deck will have a plus or minus index or a count of zero. A plus count is favorable to the player, a minus count is unfavorable. The more the count differs from zero, the greater the player's chances of winning (or losing). The player, of course, gauges the size of his bets accordingly and follows basic strategy in his playing. Later on we'll discuss the Silberstang System, which is an example of this high-low strategy.

In a more complete version of this count the player would memorize a series of strategy tables similar to those described in connection with the 10-count system. He would then have to keep both a high-low count and a tally of the total number of undealt cards left in the deck. Every time a strategic decision was required he would have to divide the deck's high-low index by the total number of undealt cards and convert this number into a decimal. This decimal number would then be used in interpreting the strategy tables as explained earlier. This approach is of course much more difficult, but also more lucrative. Sizing your bets according to the high-low index helps ensure that most of your wins will be on big bets and most of your losing hands will be on small bets. The use of the strategy tables means that you will win a larger percentage of your hands.

Because people aren't computers, blackjack systems are usually designed to provide *approximate* knowledge about the composition of the deck (e.g., 10s v. non-10s, high cards v. low). However, the more precise the player's knowledge of the make-up of the deck, the greater the percentage edge he can gain over the house. Of course, greater precision means more work. The most powerful blackjack strategies assign a specific point value to every card in the deck reflecting the degree of advantage or disadvantage that the presence of that card offers the player. Some of the best such systems have been devised by a professional blackjack player known as Lawrence Revere. Some of his systems can be found in his excellent book *Playing Blackjack as a Business.* In addition to Revere's book and the Thorp book mentioned earlier, another book that deserves the attention of any serious blackjack player is *The Casino Gambler's Guide* by Allan Wilson. It contains a complete description of the Wilson Point-count System, other current count strategies, and mathematical studies of all the standard casino games. Even if you never master an advanced count strategy, the analyses of the game, which are found in these three fine books, will make you a better blackjack player.

Counting: A Simpler Method. Counting in blackjack, as we know, means the player keeps track of exactly which cards are put into play during the course of the game. This sounds difficult, and it is. So it comes as good news to learn that even memorizing a limited number of key cards can cause a meaningful rise in percentages.

Realize that for the casino blackjack dealer the most lovely of all numbers is 5. The reason is that the dealer must draw on 16 and stand on 17. If he draws a 5 at 16 he will get 21 and beat you no matter what you hold. So the dealer just loves 5s.

On the other hand the most happy card for the player is the *ace*; without it—no blackjack, without it—no 1½ times payoff.

So, rule one: count (i.e., memorize) all the 5s and aces in play.

Adjunct to rule one: memorize all the 10-count cards as well. This means the jack, king, queen, and 10, which after the 5 and ace are the most important cards. Why? Again for the simple reason that they help make blackjacks, too.

Now, how to systematize all this? A smart player proceeds in the following way: starting with the first card played, he keeps tab, to the best of his ability, of every 5, ace, and 10-count card. This requires memorization, and at the same time as we shall see below, must be done surreptitiously (if the dealer becomes aware that he has a counter at his table he will shuffle the cards every few hands and thus stymie all counting efforts made up to that point).

How does a player count surreptitiously? There are many ways of doing it. A technique used by many is to count on the fingers. That is, every time an ace comes up, one slightly raises a finger on the right hand. Every time a 5 arrives, a finger on the left hand goes up. Ten-count cards are noted mentally on the finger joints: when the first 10-counter appears, the gambler makes note of it on the first joint of his right thumb. The second comes up and he moves the mental count to the second joint. Third time he moves the count to the first joint of the index finger, and so on. If he has prearranged it beforehand, he will automatically know the number of 10-counters simply by noting what joint he is counting at any given time. Just beware of making it too obvious. And of course beware of using such devices as a pencil and paper. They are dead giveaways.

So the counter proceeds to memorize all the 5s, aces, and 10s played until the dealer has gone approximately *halfway through the deck.* Then he stops and takes stock. How many 5s have been exposed so far? Three or more is good because it means that there is only one 5 left in the deck, a negative factor for the dealer. What about aces? There are four in the pack. Two have been played, two remain. Neither here nor there. Even money. And the 10-counters? The player recalls that only six out of the sixteen have appeared. This moves in his favor. It's two out of three: 5s and 10-counters in his favor, aces neutral. So the thing for him to do now is to bet in a liberal way. The odds are favorable.

Let's go over it again. One plays halfway through the deck, counting 5s, aces, and 10-count cards. After half the deck is gone the counter takes stock: how many have been played of four 5s, of four aces, and of sixteen 10-counters?

He makes mental calculations. If there are few 5s to come and more aces and 10-count cards, then he bets strong. If there are lots of 5s on the horizon and a minority of aces and 10s, he holds back. If it is more or less even, he plays the middle road.

Now: problems. Since the advent of Thorp and several other systems people, casinos have instituted a blackjack game with two decks rather than one, or worse, have introduced the practice of *shuffling after each hand.* The latter practice is still a bit unusual, as the casinos like to keep things moving and too many shuffles bog down the action. The two-deck system, however, seems to be catching on, and obviously having to memorize the cards from two decks is twice as hard as one. So, a bit of advice: if you are using the above counting method, make things

easier on yourself by finding a one-deck twenty-one game. They're still around.

Another important factor to consider before you attack the blackjack tables is the size of your bankroll. Remember, as we saw in the first chapter, the laws of probability hold true only in the long run. Be sure that your bankroll is large enough to ride out the long losing streak that can occur even with the best system. You need enough money to give your system a chance to work. Alternatively, make sure that your bets are small enough to make whatever funds you do have last. The great importance of a proper bank-to-bet ratio is one of the most frequently ignored factors among would-be blackjack experts.

And another tip, this one for the counting system in general: If you are using a casing method don't make it obvious. We mentioned that it is decidedly unsmart to sit at the blackjack table with pencil and paper like a stenographer. Likewise, it is harmful to become too erratic in your betting habits if you are playing a counting system. If, in fact, the counting has gone in your favor don't suddenly start plopping bets down on the table for some preposterous sum of money. People just don't do things like that, figures the dealer, unless they've got something up their sleeve. If you've been betting $1 a hand don't suddenly jump it up to $40. Double your bet perhaps, even triple it. If you're going to quadruple it, smile a lot. But don't go any further. The dealer will smell a rat.

The Silberstang System. Another interesting twenty-one system was revealed several years ago in *Playboy's Book of Games* by a writer named Edwin Silberstang. It has been used by many gamblers with much success.

Silberstang's approach is a kind of compendium of several similar systems and is quite attractive in its sim-

65

plicity. Though its mathematics are beyond our present scope, its *modus operandi* can be easily explained.

The heart of the Silberstang system is card evaluation. That is, the player gives a value to every card in play, his own, the dealer's, the other players', as many of the cards as are exposed. He does not actually memorize these cards, however. He assigns them arbitrary numerations.

Let's explain. All cards numbered 2 through 7 in the Silberstang system are arbitrarily given a numerical value of plus 1. All cards from 9 through king and ace equal minus 1. And the 8 is neutral.

Now the player begins. He looks at the cards on the board. He totals them up according to the assigned values just given. And he goes by this rule: if all the cards added and subtracted together according to the above values give him a plus score—that is, if after he has added up all the assigned values of the cards and comes out with a plus rather than a minus, then the betting is in his favor. If a minus or neutral score comes up, it is against him. On the minus counts he should then bet a minimum amount, on the plus a maximum. Simple and precise.

Further rules: when the scores add up to plus 1 or plus 2, the player should bet two chips of whatever unit value he is betting. When plus 3 or 4 he bets four chips. When plus 5 or plus 6 he bets six chips. Above plus 6 he bets eight chips. Silberstang warns, however: don't make sudden leaps in your betting habits. Don't increase your bets out of proportion to your previous rhythm of play.

Some further points:
1. When you have plus 6 or more take insurance.
2. Never split aces if you have a count of minus 6 or more, except when you are up against a low card, that is, a 2 to a 6.

3. If you have minus 6 or more and the dealer is showing a 7, 8, 9, 10, or ace *don't* double down on a hard 10. If the dealer is showing a 2 to a 6 then *do* double down on a hard 10.
4. If you have plus 6 or more, don't draw to a hard 16 or against the dealer if he is showing a 7.
5. Play two hands at a time, but no more. This gives you the advantage of seeing more cards and making more profits. Silberstang, moreover, suggests that players avoid casinos where the cards are dealt down if using this system; he points out, too, that in this case a multiple deck can be of value if dealt from a shoe, as all the cards in play will be seen.

Sucker Blackjack Systems. Two simplistic strategies employed by many ignorant players are "mimicking the dealer" and the "never-bust" strategy. Mimicking the dealer means following the same hitting and standing policy as the house: always draw to 16 and stand on 17 and never split or double down. This approach is popular because "the house does it and look how much money they make." Actually, this strategy gives the house a massive 5.7 percent edge.

The "never-bust" strategy (never drawing to a stiff) is justified on the grounds that "the house advantage derives from the automatic dealer win on a player's bust; therefore, if you never bust you eliminate the advantage." The fact is that such a player is giving the house another and much bigger advantage. This misguided thinking yields the house a 5 to 8 percent edge depending on how soft hands are played and what policy is followed on splits and double downs.

If you ever run across anybody who follows either of these strategies, don't argue with them. Just offer to play blackjack with them and make sure that you play by casino rules with you taking the part of the dealer.

A Word About Blackjack Machines

In some casinos the flesh and blood blackjack dealer has been yanked in favor of a computerized surrogate, an electronically operated blackjack machine which deals, shuffles, and psyches out opponents with the same finesse as a real live dealer. Using one of these machines, the player makes his bets via deposit and does battle with this mechanical nemesis, all in precisely the same way he would if he were playing it head-on with a dealer.

Besides dehumanizing the game of twenty-one (gambling is after all designed to be a social amusement) the blackjack machine is stacked against all comers in a way few of us would care to challenge. The major problem besetting the player is that the machine shuffles the cards after each hand, thus squelching anyone who thinks that by playing against an automaton he can bring in all his calculators, computers, and mechanical supplies. Furthermore, splitting pairs is verboten and doubling down is far more limited than at the human table. Of all gambling games, blackjack comes closest to giving the sucker a chance to beat the house edge. Why throw away this boon on a machine?

A Short Glossary for Blackjack Players

Blackjack. *An ace and 10-count card, the best hand.*

Break. *To lose.*

Burn a card. *When dealing from a single deck, to turn the first card over and place it on the bottom of the deck.*

Bust. *To exceed a count of 21 and thus to lose.*

Card counting. *Same as casing the deck.*

Casing the deck. *Memorizing cards already played.*

Count. *The numerical value of a card. Also, the sum of all cards held in one hand.*

Doubling down. *A special situation in which the house agrees to allow the player to double his bet in return for his promise to draw only one more card.*

Hard hand. *A hand in which the ace counts as 1 or in which there are no aces.*

Hit. *To take a card from the dealer. The player asks for a "hit" by saying "hit me"; or he makes a beckoning movement with his cards.*

Hole card. *The dealer's face-down card.*

Indicator card. *A card buried in the deck to mark the spot where the deck must be reshuffled.*

Insurance bet. *Betting that when the dealer shows an ace, his hole card (q.v.) will be a 10-counter, giving him a blackjack. Pays off at 2 to 1.*

Natural. *Combination of ace and a 10-count card— a blackjack.*

Pat hand. *A hand on which a player usually will not draw, i.e., from a 17 to a 20.*

Proposition bets. *Betting options reserved for the player only. Includes doubling down, insurance, and splitting pairs.*

Push. *A tie between dealer and player. A standoff (q.v.).*

Shoe. *A card box out of which the house man deals.*

Soft hand. *A hand in which the ace counts as 11.*

Split a pair. *Maneuver in which a player who has received the same two cards may play each card out as an independent hand.*

Stand. *To decline another card from the dealer.*

Standoff. *To tie. To push (q.v.).*

Stiff hand. *Any hand that can be busted by the addition of a single card, but which must still be added to in order to receive a reasonably high score, i.e. from 12 to 17.*

Poker

It's said that to be a good poker player one must be a part-time mathematician, a student of finance, an amateur psychologist, and a professional psychic. Certainly the first requisite is true. Any well-turned poker player is hip to percentages. If such an expert holds three of a kind in draw poker he knows the odds of receiving a full house are 15 to 1, not a chance worth fishing for. Or if he is sitting on four toward a fiush, he understands that chances are 4 to 1 against him. A competent player also is wise to the secrets of economics: when to bet, how much, and how. He is savvy, too, on the subject of human nature, about how people react under pressure, about how to tell when the opposition is play-acting and when it's for real. And finally, if he is really quality, the poker lover has that uncanny sixth sense for cards that helps him psych out what the other fellow is going to do and know how the cards will fall.

Although poker today is a round-the-world pastime, it's really an American card game, the great American game, in fact, ranked several notches higher in popularity than its only competitor, contract bridge. Though its origins are obscure, chances are it was devised somewhere in the eastern desert kingdoms, probably in Persia, for a Persian game called *an-nas* bears the modern game more than a coincidental resemblance. It came to Europe, historians believe, with returning crusaders and by 1700 it was a common round in every tavern and alehouse. One version of this oriental diversion was the game of *pochen* in Germany. Another was the still-played English brag. In France card players anted-up in a contest called *poque*. This last version, the French version, was the one that would capture the fancy of Americans. *Poque* migrated to the States with French settlers. In 1803, after the Louisiana Purchase, English-speaking gamesters quickly picked it up. They modified it, Americanized it, claimed it for their own.

The origin of the name "poker" is peculiarly American. Almost as soon as *poque* arrived in the United States it became part of every Mississippi gambler's repertoire. Now most river-going gentlemen, we know, were Southerners born and raised, with accents as thick as jam on bread. Not able to *parler français,* these high-class hustlers nonetheless had to somehow pronounce the name of the new-fangled foreigner's game, and they did so with incomparable fractured French. *Poque* quickly became *poo-kah.* For over a generation this was the accepted pronunciation. But the metamorphosis was not over. During the early years of the Civil War, Yankees and Rebels occasionally fraternized during a lull in the battle. Their favorite pastime was cards, and during these sessions poker began its first infiltration of the North. The card-rattling Yankees with their short-clipped, nasal accents then proceeded to reduce rather than drawl out the vowels, changing the *ah* to *er* and the *poo* back to *po*. In the end the game was no longer *poo-kah* but *pok-er.*

The number of poker games in existence today are uncountable, a majority of them boasting some of the most colorful names in gambling such as butcher boy, lame brain, spit-in-the-ocean, wild widow, big sol. However, when one gets down to it, there are really only two basic pokers: draw and stud. In draw, all cards are dealt face down. In stud, most of the cards are exposed.

Draw poker is the older and more popular of the two poker games. It can be played by as many as ten, though five or six make the ideal match. The object is for one player to win the pot by showing a higher ranking hand than all the others. Before the game begins, players decide on betting procedure. They can practice "fixed limits," in which bets cannot exceed a previously agreed

*The final round of the
Third World Series of Poker
included perennial favorite Amarillo
Slim (l), Puggy Pearson (r), and
Texas Doyle (center r), who
later cashed in due to fatigue.*

amount; "pot limit," where a player can wager no more than the amount in the pot at the time of his bet; or "table stakes," an approximation of the legendary "sky's the limit" game of millionaires, where each player's limit is the number of chips belonging to him at the beginning of the deal.

In draw poker most people play "jackpots," in which a player in order to open must hold at least a pair of jacks or better. After the opening bet is made each player must decide if he is going to "pass," that is, drop out of the betting (and sometimes the game); "call," or match the money already bet; or "raise"—meet the pre-vious bet and then increase it. Although rules differ from game to game, if the other players cannot or will not meet the raise they usually must drop the hand, and the higher bettor takes the pot *regardless* of the cards he holds. (If, indeed, he didn't have a good hand but was betting as if he did, he was using the most ingenious play in the gambler's bag of tricks, the "bluff.")

The players now draw from the pack to improve their hands. Another betting session takes place with the same call-and-raise system. Finally, there is a "show-down," in which the highest ranking hand is declared, and the winner takes the pot.

An interesting and challenging variation of draw poker is lowball. In this version the *lowest* hand wins the pot. Thus, a hand like a full house which would normally be very desirable is to be avoided at all costs. Aces are played low and straights and flushes do not count. The perfect hand in lowball would be an A-2-3-4-5. This hand is known as the "wheel" or the "bicycle." Betting and drawing are the same as in regular draw poker.

The game of stud poker, once so popular in Prohibition America, today is seldom played in penny-ante games but is still a favorite among high rollers and professional poker players. It is governed by the same rules and the same card values as draw poker. The difference is that in five- or seven-card stud each player is dealt one face-down card and a series of face-up cards rather than five down cards.

The game of five-card stud begins with each player being dealt a face-down and face-up card. A betting interval follows, with the player who holds the best face-up cards wagering first. Three more rounds follow, each with a single face-up card dealt to each player and each with a betting interval in between. After the fourth and last betting round comes the showdown. Each player exposes his hole card and the highest hand wins.

Variations on stud abound. There is seven-card stud in which each player is dealt two hole cards and a face-up card. This is followed by a round of betting. There is one more face-up card followed by a round of betting, another face-up card and round of betting, and one last face-up card and round of betting. Finally there is one face-down card and a last round of betting. For the showdown each player selects the best five out of seven cards to represent his hand. High-low poker, another variant, is played with the highest ranking hand and the lowest ranking hand splitting the pot, the lowest being 7-5-4-3-

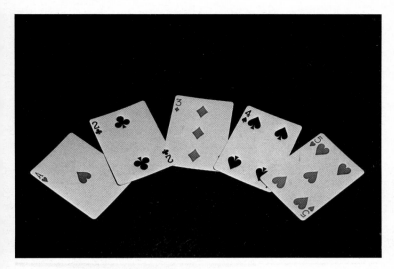

Odds Against Improving an Original Hand in Draw Poker			
Original Hand	No. of Cards Drawn	Improved Hand	Odds Against
One pair	3	2 pairs	5.25 to 1
	3	3 of a kind	7.7 to 1
	3	full house	97 to 1
	3	4 of a kind	359 to 1
	2	2 pairs	17 to 1
	2	3 of a kind	11.9 to 1
	2	full house	119 to 1
	2	4 of a kind	1080 to 1
Two pairs	1	full house	11 to 1
Three of a kind	2	full house	15 to 1
	2	4 of a kind	22.5 to 1
	1	full house	15 to 1
Four straight (open)	1	straight	5 to 1
Four straight (gap)	1	straight	11 to 1
Four flush	1	flush	4.5 to 1
Three flush	2	flush	23 to 1
Two flush	3	flush	97 to 1
Four straight flush (open)	1	straight flush	22.5 to 1
	1	any straight or flush	2 to 1
Four straight flush (gap)	1	straight flush	46 to 1
	1	any straight or flush	3 to 1

2. High-low seven-card stud goes by the same rules, with the players allowed to choose the best or worst five out of seven cards in their hand.

A Few Fine Points of Poker

Poker can be learned in a night, just like chess. But like chess, a person can spend his whole life playing it without getting very good. To play good poker requires a number of skills. A few of them are natural gifts like a good memory, resilient nerves, and a logical thought process. Most of them can be acquired, however, and until they are acquired no one can call himself a pro. What to do to become good at poker? Here are a few suggestions:

Learn the Odds. Learning the odds at poker is a prerequisite for good play. This may sound like a sizeable job, but if you are a regular poker player the few hours invested in committing the odds to memory will be a minuscule labor when compared with the number of hours you will spend at the poker table. Think of how much these few hours will profit your winnings.

On every play of the game in poker the mathematics change. It is these mathematics that determine the probability of getting or not getting a certain hand. This may seem obvious, but it is a fact that this simple axiom is too often neglected by the poker addict who thinks his luck will guide him through. Suppose a player has a pair of 8s. He decides to hold a kicker—that is, a third card—on the hopes that he will draw himself two pairs. How are the odds behind such a choice? If he knew them he wouldn't hold so tight to his kicker. For the odds tell him that if a player has a pair it's 2½-to-1 against his drawing another pair; while at the same time, if he retains the kicker it's 8-to-1 that he'll draw a card to match it and get two pairs. The folly of keeping the kicker is now obvious; but more obvious is the fact that if the player

Survival of the fittest. Horseshoe Casino's annual World Series of Poker in Las Vegas began with 22 men, each buying in for $10,000, and continued until one was victorious in this winner-take-all game.

knew these odds in advance he wouldn't have even considered holding onto a third card in the first place. Of course, the player may be planning to bluff by indicating he has three of a kind. This might work, depending on his knowledge of the other players and the general course of the previous betting.

Another example: suppose a player is holding a four-card straight open in the middle. What are his possibilities of getting the fifth card? He doesn't know. He's in the dark. It's the wrong way to play poker. If he knew he'd know that the chances of getting what he needs with a four-card straight open in the middle are 1 in 11.8; and if by chance he is holding a four-card straight flush open in the middle the chances are 1 in 47 of getting the fifth card. The greenhorn, of course, receiving four such beautiful cards finds it hard not to gamble for the fifth. Of course, there are another eight cards that would give him a flush and another three that would give him a straight. But the seasoned poker player knows exactly what these odds are and takes into account the amount of money in the pot and the amount he would have to pay for the outdraw.

When You're Beat, Drop Out. If you're in a game of stud and you're holding a pair of queens this generally means you'll take the pot. But poker is a game for the flexible and for those who can bend with every wind. Just because you're holding queens doesn't mean you should get complacent. The minute you see your opponent has something higher, kings perhaps, then play it smart and drop out. The odds say you're going to lose. Remain loose and wait for the next hand. Poker is a game for the patient.

This also holds true with the better hands, of course. The exhilaration of receiving three-of-a-kind or something even better can make a player heady. He feels

Masters of logic, shrewd observers of other players' every move, these men are in fierce competition for one week or more. Advisors can help with strategy, as below.

confident, so confident, in fact, that he forgets there are other players in the game. The minute another player gives an indication that he has something better, *no matter how good your hand is* it is best to fold and fight another day.

Learn to Observe Others. Psychology should never be underestimated in poker. Everyone knows about the poker face, about remaining inscrutable no matter what crisis may arise. But there's more to it than that. By making a concerted effort to play heads-up poker at every possible moment one can gain remarkably great amounts of information in a remarkably short time.

For example, some players have an unremitting urge to tell everybody at the table what kind of cards they're holding. It's all done nonverbally, of course, and is completely unconscious on the part of the doer. Maybe it's an unconscious urge to lose, maybe just a case of the uncools, who knows? Whatever the reason, take advantage of it. Look for players whose mannerisms tip off their intent. Harvey L., an inveterate poker player and inveter-

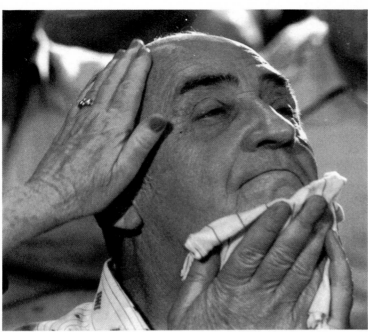

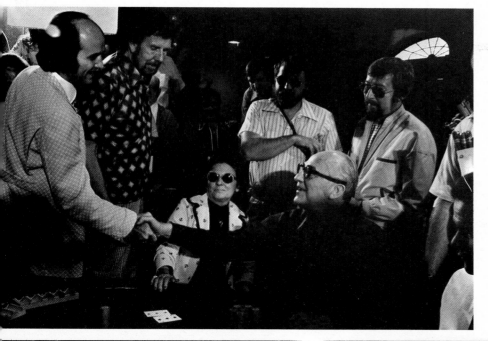

Tension mounts as stakes increase until one survivor remains. The winner gets a round of applause, a toast with champagne, and entire the pot.

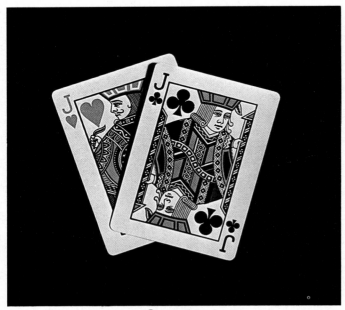

One pair

Two pairs

ate loser as well, finally came close to despair over his unfortunate poker game. Harvey knew the odds, had plenty of game experience. He knew he was a better poker player than anyone in his every Wednesday night group. And still he lost. Ernie Z., a close friend of his and a successful poker player since college days, finally agreed to sit in on a Wednesday night game with Harvey and psych out his problem.

In less than ten minutes Ernie saw the dilemma. It was simple. Every time Harvey was dealt an interesting hand he immediately began to blink. The better the hand the faster his lids pulsated. The habit was totally unconscious on Harvey's part and quite obvious to his opponents. Because of his mannerism, Harvey lost enough money to pay for several mortgages plus a pair of eyeglasses.

The lesson is clear. Be on the lookout for those subliminal giveaways like a change in facial coloring, a shift or squint of the eyes, a raising or lowering of the voice, a clenching of the hands. Look for repeating habits. Get to know the people you play with. People are often an open book at the poker table—if only we have eyes to decipher them.

Know Basic Strategy. There are certain moves in a poker game you make and there are certain ones you don't make. If you are in a game of seven-card stud and you're not holding several high cards, then fold. If you're holding anything less than a pair in a game of draw poker, then fold. If given the opportunity, open the pot no matter what hand you're holding. Don't get into fixed betting habits; your opposition will soon learn them and take advantage. Try to avoid bluffing when there are more than three players in the pot—one of them is bound to keep you honest. But don't be afraid to bluff occasionally; if you've bluffed and there are no callers at the end of the

Three of a kind

Straight

Flush

Full house

Four of a kind

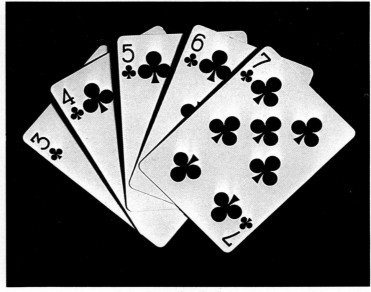

Straight flush

Poker enthusiasts need not be professionals, playing games with thousand-dollar pots, to have fun. Most poker takes place at home, where runs for beer, sandwiches, and cigarettes can be made.

play don't expose your hand. (Why give your opponents valuable psychological information about yourself if you don't have to?) These are of course just a few of the many examples of poker strategy. What is important is that one be thoroughly familiar with all of them. Do this by playing a lot, by reading, studying, observing. Know your game. **Be Savvy.** What is poker savvy? Things like this: avoiding poker games when the odds are too high for your wallet; not advising or kibitzing other players while a game is in progress; learning how to handle cards well and not being a sloppy dealer or a card-dropper (not only are these habits annoying, but they will make fellow players suspicious of cheating); not complaining when you lose, not crowing when you win; avoiding alcohol when you play; and learning to leave gracefully when you realize you are in over your head.

Monolog by a Poker Shark

Sam P. has been playing poker for many a year and he tells us that he's come out on top doing it.

Sam has agreed to give some of his trade dialog, some of the smart tactics he's learned from hard, bloody experience. Maybe Sam's not giving us his deepest insights—people rarely disclose their real secrets, no matter how much they may protest to the contrary—but with a little practice the poker player can turn the following information into dollars and cents.

"Poker? Yeah, poker's my game. It's the best. Don't let anyone tell you it's not a game of skill. I make a nice living at it, and I know lots of other guys who do too. I even had one pal of mine clobber a sucker who insisted poker was all luck. But anyway . . . what can I tell you? Anything I say you can read in a book. Trouble is then you'll go out and gamble with someone who knows what

he's doing and you'll forget everything you've read. Hey, that's good, that's your first lesson: read all the books, then forget them, forget rule one, rule two, rule three. Just play according to the style you like best.

"But, anyway, you want some information. A lot of the classic rules come to mind. Best hand before the draw usually wins. Don't bet unless you're holding jacks or better. When you know you're holding losers, drop quick. That's old stuff, isn't it? What else comes to mind? If I had to give the best advice I know, it's to know as much as you can about the people you're playing with. That old saying you see quoted all over the poker books about how a poker player has to be a psychologist is true. Everybody's got a different personality, you see, and it comes out when you play poker with them. If a guy is crazy he'll probably be a crazy bettor at poker. I say probably, because there are no hard rules. If some stiff is tight-assed, he'll probably play poker the same way. Then, once you see what kind of poker he plays, play that way back at him. If he plays tight, you play tight. If he plays crazy, get a little crazy yourself, you understand? Do you understand why I'm saying that? Because otherwise you'll get hurt. Because let's say you're in a game with five lunatics all raising as if it was the last game they'd play before they croaked. And you're there playing it nice and safe, not betting on anything worse than aces. What happens? They ante you to death. Every pot you're losing ante, right? Pot after pot. And that can cost you. And then, Mister Big, you finally get something nice, three ladies, for example, and you start betting like crazy. Everyone knows you've got something nice so they drop. You're out in the cold. Of course, this kind of situation *can* be the kind of stuff first-rate poker is made of, but you have to know what you're doing to make it that way. Let's suppose you get into a game with some wild players. You

let them toss their dough around for a while and you just sit tight, playing it close to the chest. Then all of a sudden you start betting high. You're really holding crap, you see, but you bluff it. Some of the players think you're really strong and they leave the game. A few will keep raising though. You raise them back so high and recklessly that they figure you're so conservative that you wouldn't do this unless you had good cards. So they scare and finally drop too. Maybe you don't make a gigantic winning, but what you do is to throw them off their stride. They thought they had you pegged and you fooled them. And the best thing you can do with a good player is to let him think he's pegged you, then throw him a great big curve. A confused poker player is a lousy poker player. Remember that. That's psychology.

"You want a lot of simple rules. But there are no simple rules. That's a rule itself. Play each hand individu-ally and don't keep thinking back to, 'Hey, what would Oswald Jacoby or someone like that do now?' Each hand is different. And that makes me think: each bet is differ-ent, too. Don't think of the last bet you made when you're making this one. Each bet has nothing to do with the last one. They're independent, you understand? If you've been losing all night don't let that stop you from betting high on a particular hand if it's good. The fact that your luck has been rotten up to this point doesn't mean your luck will be bad on this hand. Don't play scared poker, either. Scared poker means that when you're betting you don't go all the way. You remember that you have high grocery bills or something and you get frightened and pull back. If you're going to do it, then do it. Don't be a half-ass. On the other hand, there's smart poker, too. This means that when you know you're licked you drop out without having to prove how brave you are.

In friendly but serious poker, five men battle over one pile of chips after another. Such casual late-night games often capture players' attention until early next morning.

This hand is a winner. A full house can only be beaten by royal flush, straight flush, and four of a kind. But don't forget that such a hand does not guarantee you'll win—it can be bluffed out before showdown.

"Another rule: count the number of players in the game. That sounds funny, doesn't it? You see, some jerks don't realize that the number of players affects the odds. 'What's the matter with you, stupid,' I say to these guys. 'If you're holding queens in a game of draw with four others, your chances of winning aren't that bad. But that same hand in a game with seven players won't get you across the street.' Queens just don't make it in a big game, you understand. The reason is simple. It's the odds. If you're under the gun in a seven-man game with aces, open. But don't do it with queens. And you probably shouldn't do it with kings either, though lots of people will give you an argument on this. At any rate, pay attention to the number of people in the game.

"What else can I tell you? Some of my friends ask me how to deal with players who draw a single card. That's a legitimate question. Maybe they're fishing for a flush or straight, or maybe they're just bluffing me. What should I do? Well, you know, whatever he's trying for, the chances are pretty bad that he's going to get it, whether it's a straight, flush, or full-boater. Odds-wise he's probably going to miss, so it's a pretty good bet to bet against him, even if he starts raising like hell after the draw. You'll find out that way if he's a bluffer, and that's an important thing to know about anyone. Bluffers are addicts. They can't stop bluffing. Everytime they bluff they think it's for the first time, and that it's going to fool you 'cause it's so unusual. Even if they've bluffed a hundred times already they still think it will be a surprise. Don't ask me why it's like that, but it is. Once a bluffer, always a bluffer. A really smart player plays it close most of the time, then throws in a bluff. Then back to conservative play. Then later another bluff, maybe a couple in a string. That's good poker, at least as far as I'm concerned. Keep them off balance.

"My advice to the poker player is this: Stay away from the sharks. They're good, really good, much better than you can believe. Don't think you can fool them by playing some weird style either. They know all the tricks better than you. Some people think poker is a game of luck, and that they can fool the good players. Do you know what? I tell the people who say that that they're nuts!"

A Few Vital Poker Statistics

Like all games, poker depends on the percentages, some of which are supplied here. So here for study or memorization are some very important odds that all good poker players know:

Possible Poker Hands		
Hand	Number Possible	Chance of Receiving
Straight flush	40	1 in 64,974
Four of a kind	626	1 in 4165
Full House	3744	1 in 695
Flush	5108	1 in 509
Straight	10,200	1 in 256
Three of a kind	54,912	1 in 48
Two pairs	123,552	1 in 21
One pair	1,098,240	1 in 2.5

Uncle George on Draw Poker

Uncle George is a mythical character, a mouthpiece invented by a nineteenth-century poker expert and shark. Lounging back in his armchair, spilling forth advice to his greenhorn nephew about how to avoid being cheated at poker, George is the perfect kibitzer. Fact is, though, Uncle George and the gambler who wrote the book know their stuff. The information they reveal here is as valuable as it was a century ago.

"I begin by repeating the advice of the father to his son," muses Uncle George. "Said he, 'my son, if you play cards for gain, you will surely lose in the end; but if you will see that the cards are *cut* immediately before dealing every time, your money will last you longer.' This was good advice, and just as good now as when first given. There are card players who can shuffle cards so adroitly as to 'put up a hand' right before your eyes, and you not know it. Even a bungler can shuffle so as to give himself a pair, or at least to have knowledge of what cards are left on the top or bottom of the pack, which knowledge he can make useful in many ways. For instance, after the deal, he finds in looking at his hand that he has a pair that match the card he knows is on the bottom of the pack. In helping himself, he takes this bottom card; he does his work so fine you cannot discover the cheat. And if he has a 'four straight,' a 'four flush' or 'two pairs,' and the bottom card will fill his hand, he takes it, as I have said, making his straight or flush or full. Many other points under this head could be given you, my boy, why the cards should be cut the last thing before being dealt. Strictly, the blank card of the pack should always be the bottom card of the pack before being dealt.

"Whenever the cards are cut, be sure you have two separated parts of the pack put together before deal-

Second most popular game in the casino,
blackjack requires skill and good judgment to play well.
It has become a favorite because the expert player
can turn the house edge (18 percent for terrible play)
to a player advantage of 2.3 percent. Most successful
players follow a card counting or casing system.

ing. The party shuffling has a chance to know what cards are on the top of the pack, and by holding only the cut portion in his hand while dealing, knows into whose hand these cards fall, or if they should fall to himself, he would know how to discard, so as to have his hand helped by drawing. You see this gives the dealer an advantage over the other players.

"The pack, or any undealt portions of it, should at all times remain in sight of the players, and *upon the table* and held by the dealer only while actually engaged in dealing or helping hands. This prevents the dealer from obtaining knowledge while holding the cards on or below the surface of the table.

"In gathering up the discard cards for the purpose of shuffling, be sure that the faces of the cards are turned from the shuffler: otherwise the party shuffling gains an advantage by knowing the position of some of the higher cards, and besides, it gives him an opportunity of 'putting up the cards' while shuffling. In no instance, however, should the discarded cards be gathered up while some are still engaged in playing their hands.

"In helping the players after discarding, always give the number called for, together as they come from the pack, and not *singly*, one by one; for this reason: there are persons who can with their fingernails, or ring, or by a slight bend, so mark the cards, as to know them whenever these marks are seen; and in dealing they can only see the marks by dealing the cards off one at a time, and not together. And besides, if the dealer deals them off *singly*, and knows the bottom card, he can, as I have said, help himself to that card, which he could not so well do by dealing them off together. Again, some dealers are so expert, that they can deal continually the *second card* from the top of the pack; they can give you any number called for, *one at a time* without disturbing the top card, which

top card the dealer, of course, wants himself, to help his hand. This could not be done if the number called for were dealt off together and not one at a time. This is called 'dealing seconds.'

"Always look with suspicion upon one who wears eyeglasses while playing, and who wears them at no other time; or upon the player who habitually calls for more light—who wants the gas turned on, and the window shades raised, when there is sufficient light already. Our playing cards are large print. A man nearly blind can distinguish the cards, and ordinary eyes can read them distinctly at twilight. In such cases the probabilities are, that the one desiring more light is dealing with marked cards; the marks are so fine that strong light and magnifying glasses are necessary to see the marks. I say, my boy, you must keep a sharp look-out for all such players.

"Look out for the player who is continually fussing with the pack. I think it is called 'monkeying with the cards.' The probabilities are that he is 'putting them up.'

"Look out for that player who invariably, when he picks up the pack to deal, looks at the bottom card, or shows it to the player at his left. Also for the one who is always precise in cutting the cards at some particular place in the pack. These are all indications of the party's trying to take advantage, and must be looked upon with suspicion. The last is called 'cutting to the break.'

"Watch very closely the *uneasy* player, one who is almost constantly on the move; using the cuspidor often, though neither smoking nor chewing; his hands and arms continually on the move, while they ought to be quiet on, or above the table. The probabilities are that such a player is taking cards from the pack, and secreting them in some place on his person—inside his neck collar, under his handkerchief, in his lap, up his coatsleeve, or holding them in the bend of his knee, and using whatever the

Text continued on page 97

Craps is said to be the fastest gambling game ever invented, and indeed the most noise and excitement in the casino emanate from the crap table. Left: Serious players are able to concentrate in the midst of even the most sense-stimulating games. Such players will refuse the free drinks occasionally offered by the casino, unless they are in the game for casual fun, like those below.

The roulette wheel—a universal symbol of fate—
is actually a beautifully constructed piece of equipment.
The dealer spins it counter-clockwise and then spins
the ball clockwise around the rim of the wheel.
Below: The player is making a corner bet—that is, placing the
chips at the junction of four corners. It pays 8 to 1.

Baccarat has traditionally exuded an aura of elegance and
big money. The multitude of regulations and special
terminology can be intimidating to the beginner, but actually the game is
completely mechanical, and the dealer will make sure
the rules are followed. Bottom r: Chemin de fer, a game similar to
baccarat, is seldom encountered in American casinos.

hand dealt him can be benefited thereby. At other times, two or three cards of like denomination are held in the palm of the hand to be used with the next hand given, in helping to make a very large hand."

Baccarat

Baccarat was introduced to American bettors sometime during the end of the last century. Two related but different games are chemin de fer and baccarat banque. To say that baccarat never really caught on would not be wholly accurate, though it never was (and probably never will be) competition for its not-so-distant cousin, blackjack.

Baccarat, you see, is a game for the rich. *The very rich.* Most bets start at $20 and end at $2,000, and all bets are made in hard cash.

There's another reason though for baccarat's exclusiveness, which John Scarne amusingly explains in *Scarne on Cards:* "The game's relative infrequency is due mainly to the size and cost of its equipment. It requires a heavy kidney-shaped table, its surface juicily padded and painted, with a built-in money drawer and discard cylinder: price, according to my latest catalog from a concern in the Midwest, $165. It requires a six-deck dealing box looking like a cranberry scoop that has gone society: $10 for the American model, $27.50 for the French, in black walnut with chromium-silver finish. The croupier, squatting in the concavity of the kidney table, needs an ebony-finish pallet to slide the cash and cards around: five bucks." The area surrounding the table is roped off in order to keep the hoi polloi from mixing in. The dealers and the customers are, for the most part, formally and the latter expensively attired.

Although the beginner at baccarat may stand with gaping jaw before the multifold *do*'s and *don't*'s of the game, in truth it is one of the most automatic and skill-less of all banking games, the reason being that all strategy is fixed by house rules beforehand. The player is told when to hit, stand, and so forth, and so all he must do is receive his cards, follow the printed rules on display, pray, and let the croupier do the rest. Sounds ultramechanical, perhaps, but then so does the slot machine; and at a 1.15 percent house advantage compared to a 40 to 70 percent edge for the slots, one can see where the better risk lies.

In baccarat the suits have no significance. The honor cards and the 10s count zero, the aces 1, and all others equal their own numerical value. Several decks are used, shuffled by one of the players, reshuffled by the croupier, marked in the bottom with a blank card, and dealt out of a shoe. The object of the game is to get a combination of cards that totals 9 or as close to it as possible. Unlike blackjack, it is never possible to bust, since anything over 9 simply equals the second digit, i.e., a 13 counts as 3, a 17 as 7, a 15 as 5, and so forth.

Baccarat is played around a curved table with numbered slots on the layout to mark each player's seat number. At the start of the game the player seated at number-one slot starts the action, dealing two face-down cards to himself and two to the croupier. (The hand the player deals to the croupier is the player hand and the hand he deals to himself is the bank hand.) Players at the table then have the chance to bet either on the bank or on the player. (The first time a bank hand loses, the deal will pass to the player on the dealer's right—this is the principal difference between baccarat and baccarat banque, for in the latter the house serves as dealer for the entire game.) After the deal the cards are turned over and the card count dictates whether the dealer and player receive a third card. Here, as mentioned, the rules are ironclad. In Las Vegas they are as follows:

Sit back and relax. Decisions are made for you, rules are inflexible in baccarat, but odds aren't bad. Fortunes are made and lost, all in an air of refinement. Below: Hands are dealt from a box or "shoe."

Baccarat Rules				
Player Hand Rules		**Bank Hand Rules**		
Having		**Having**	draws when player draws	stands when player draws
0,1,2,3,4,5	Draws a card	3	1,2,3,4,5,6,7,9,10	8
6,7	Stands	4	2,3,4,5,6,7	1,8,9,10
8,9	Natural—bank cannot draw	5	4,5,6,7	1,2,3,8,9,10
		6	6,7	
Pictures and tens do not count		7	stands	
Always wait		8,9	natural—player cannot draw	
for the dealer's instructions		*bank hand stands with 6 when player hand stands with 6 or 7*		

Chemin de fer, popular posh European banking game similar to baccarat, claims 40 tables in Deauville Casino, has been played since 17th century.

After the action is finished, if the player's count is closer to 9 than the banker's, he wins; if not, he loses. In case of ties, it is a standoff and a new hand is dealt. Such, very briefly, is an outline of the game of baccarat, the money game *par excellence*.

A Word About Faro

Popular taste in gambling entertainment changes as fast as the morning headlines. Not even a hundred years ago faro was the world's most popular card game. Men lived and died around the casino's conspicuous tiger portrait, a giant painting that announced a faro game in progress; here a man could come to "buck the tiger." Dostoevsky built one of the most dramatic episodes of *The Brothers Karamazov* around a faro match; in *War and Peace* this was the game at which Count Rostof lost his family fortune; faro was a favorite of riverboat gamblers, of New York City slickers, of Serbian counts, and South American gauchos. But now, today, just try to find a game. You're lucky if you'll see half a dozen in the entire state of Nevada.

When you find it you'll quickly realize that faro is not exactly a game of skill. In fact the only real talent needed is in the betting, which is made at a layout. Enameled on it are the thirteen cards of the suit of spades. Essentially the gambler is at the mercy of the dealer's card box that holds a shuffled pack of cards. The dealer takes the first card from this box, cryptically termed "soda," sets it aside, draws another that is designated the "loser," another that is the "winner," and so forth back and forth on each turn. The player then bets on whether each card will win or lose. If the dealer turns two consecutive cards of matching value, he gets half of what is bet on that card.

For the modern gambler the disappearance of faro

is a sad affair. The odds at this game are rather splendid when compared to a lot of other casino diversions and are even as good as the best of blackjack and craps. But be of good cheer. The game *can* be found; you just have to persevere.

Gin Rummy

Since its introduction in the 1930s, gin rummy has been a favorite social game. In recent years it has increased in popularity among big-money gamblers. Poker champion Amarillo Slim recently admitted that these days he plays more high-stakes gin rummy than poker. The essential rules of the game may be summarized as follows:

Play

Only two players may participate in a hand. To start the game, each player draws a card to determine the dealer. Generally the loser deals. The players agree after the start what the game-winning total will be. Each player is dealt ten cards. The remainder of the deck is placed on the table to form the stock and the top card is placed face up beside it to begin the discard pile. (Some play with eleven cards dealt to the nondealer, who begins the discard pile by discarding one card from his hand.)

The object of the game is to reduce one's point count of unmatched cards by forming "melds" of three- or four-of-a-kind or three or more cards of the same suit in sequence. To accomplish this, each player in turn draws either the top card of the stock or the face card of the discard pile and then discards one card face up onto the discard pile. If on his first turn the nondealer does not wish to draw the up card, he must give the dealer the option to do so before proceeding. A player may not discard the card he just drew from the discard pile on the same turn. Examination of the discard pile is forbidden.

End of Play

Play continues until one player either "knocks" or "goes gin." A player may knock, after drawing and before discarding, whenever his total of unmatched points is ten or less. (In computing unmatched points, picture cards count ten each; aces count one; all other cards count their index value.)

When a player knocks, he discards face down and each player then lays down his melds face up and his unmelded cards in a separate group. The knocker's opponent may "lay off" any unmelded cards in his hand that match the knocker's melds. The point values of each player's unmatched cards are then totaled and the difference determines the score as explained below. The loser generally deals the next hand.

A player need not exercise his option to knock. He may instead continue playing in the hopes of going gin. A player has gin when all ten cards in his hand are arranged in melds. When a player goes gin, play is concluded as explained above except that the loser may not lay off cards against the winning hand.

If no one has knocked or gone gin by the time the stock is down to two cards, the hand is declared a draw. The dealer of the previous hand deals the next one.

Scoring

If a player's knock is successful (his opponent's unmelded points are higher than his) he receives the difference in unmelded points between himself and his opponent plus a "box" bonus of 25 points for winning the hand. If, however, the opponent's unmelded points are equal to or lower than the knocker's, the opponent is said to have "undercut" and receives the difference in points plus a

25-point undercut bonus as well as the box bonus.

If a player goes gin he receives the total of his opponent's unmelded points plus a gin bonus of 25 points and the box bonus.

Play continues until one player scores the agreed game total or more. If the agreed total was 100, the winning player receives a game bonus of 100 points and wins the difference in points between the two scores. The bonus is always the game-winning total. If the loser has not scored at all during the game the winner doubles the entire score.

Finally, keep in mind that variations in the scoring of bonuses are common. Players should make sure that they are agreed on the ground rules *before* play begins.

There are a number of variations of the game. When there are three players, one is captain (by pick of the highest card). The second highest plays against the captain until he loses. Then the third player takes his place until he loses. The second player comes back, and so on until the end of the game. The captain wins from both the other players or loses to both. The same principle holds true wherever there is an odd number of players. The most common variations are Oklahoma Gin and Hollywood. In Oklahoma Gin, play is exactly the same as in the standard game except that the value of the first card of the discard pile determines the knocking number. Thus, if the up card is a 7, a player must have 7 unmatched points or less to knock. (If, however, the up card is an ace, the players must go for gin.) In addition, if the card is a spade, the scoring on that hand is doubled.

In Hollywood only the scoring differs from the regular game. In effect, three games are scored simultaneously. The score sheet contains three double columns, one for each game. The first hand won by each player is entered only in game one. His second winning hand is entered in games one and two; his third winning hand and all subsequent wins are credited in all three games. When either player reaches the agreed winning total or more points in a game, that game is ended and no more scores are entered in it, but play goes on in the other games until they reach the winning total of points.

Team play is very popular. There may be two, three, or four on a side. In some games one team sits on one side of the table, the other on the opposite side. In this variation the players on each team may look at his partner's hand or hands if there are more than two on a team. Most team play is by alternate arrangement—one from Team A sits next to one from Team B and so on. The members of a team do not see each other's cards. The strategy in team play is much more complex than in head-to-head play, as we shall see.

Strategy

There is a great deal more to gin strategy than the average player realizes. Most players think that because they remember a few of the discards they are playing a good game. They continually make the same fundamental errors and then blame the results on poor cards. They may even emerge victorious when matched against equally unskilled players, and this only reinforces their bad playing habits. The following advice can go a long way toward making an average player a superior one.

Get on Score (Fast). Your first priority in every game should be to get on score as soon as possible, even if it's with only a couple of points. This is your insurance against that 100-point shutout penalty. A player who passes up an early opportunity to knock in an attempt to go gin is risking losing the game (not to mention the box bonus) in the hopes of winning a 25-

point gin bonus. That just doesn't make sense. Don't assume that if you blow it on the first hand you can always play it cautious and go for an early knock the next hand. If the cards start to go against you, you may not get another chance to score for the rest of the game. The only prudent policy is to get on the score pad on the very first opportunity.

Play to Knock (Fast). The single most common error of the average gin player is to try to go gin on most of his hands. Every really expert gin player knows that the way to win at gin is to go out as soon as possible. Most big scores at gin are won by an early knock that catches your opponent with a fistful of unmatched cards. Even if you only catch him with a few points, you still win the box bonus—and box bonuses are usually the most important factor in scoring. The only situation when you should try for gin is when the game has progressed to a late stage. In such a case, if you were to knock you would run a serious risk of an undercut.

And once you are in a position to knock, don't dally for a couple of picks out of curiosity as to what might develop. Remember, every time you buy a card, your opponent gets one also. Every time you give him a crack at the deck, you give him another chance to complete a meld and thus reduce his count by 15 or 20 points or more.

Maintain a Knock Reserve. If your goal is to knock as soon as possible, your strategy should reflect that goal. An important element in that strategy is your knock reserve. Try to get and hold on to one, two, or three low cards which total less than the knock card. Then if you fill your meld possibilities you can go out immediately and avoid the agony of having to draw card after card in an effort to reduce your count to ten or under while your opponent continues to improve his hand.

Don't Speculate. In gin rummy argot, speculation means drawing a card from the discard pile which does not complete or add to a meld but which does create another meld possibility. Don't do it. Your first priority is to fill the meld possibilities you already have. When you draw from the discard pile you pass up a draw from the stock that might have allowed you to create a meld.

Besides, when you draw from the discard pile to create a possibility you notify your opponent as to what you need, making it far less likely that your new meld possibility will ever be filled. Even with a poor hand you are better off letting new meld possibilities develop from the stock. At least that way you don't tip off the opposition.

Don't Throw Live Cards. If you can possibly avoid it (and you can't always), don't throw your opponent a card he may be able to use. Remember what cards have been discarded and always make discards with an eye to safety. This more than anything else is the key to expert gin play. If you have a five and an eight in your deadwood and you know that the five is safe while the eight is wild, discard the five. The three-point reduction in your hand isn't worth the risk of allowing your opponent to make a meld that will reduce his count by about 20 points or more. Don't be penny-wise and pound-foolish. Even breaking up a meld possibility is a sacrifice worth making in this situation. It may hurt but it's the smart play.

Team Play. The most important thing in team play is to keep alert to the score situation. If your partner has won 45 points you must direct your play to get under 20 points. Even if you are sure that playing a 10 will give your opponent gin, do so if that gets you under 20. Then your team will win the hand and get 2 extra box bonuses. On the other hand, if your partner has lost 45 points,

giving your opponents the game score by 20 points, you must try for gin. Winning a few points will not save the game. Even if you lost the hand, your consolation is that the game itself was lost anyway.

In team play it is best to knock as soon as you can. This will give your partner an edge if you win. If you lose he will know how to direct his play. The general axiom is "second man down." If you are ahead or behind a modest number of points after the first hand is decided, knock as soon as you can so that the remaining partner will know what to do and what the chances are.

There are any number of situations in team play where knowing the score will enable you to use common sense in determining whether to reduce your hand as quickly as possible, whether to play for gin, or whether to take long chances. Pay attention to the score!

Pinochle

Auction pinochle is the most popular form of the game. However, other versions include two-handed pinochle, which has lost popularity in recent years to gin rummy, and partnership pinochle, which is played with many variations throughout the country.

Rules of Auction Pinochle

The game may be played by three, four, or five players, only three of whom participate in any one hand. A deck consisting of two aces, kings, queens, jacks, tens, and nines of each suit is employed. Each player is dealt fifteen cards with three cards dealt in the center of the table to form the "widow." Various procedures are followed in dealing the cards—the most common is to deal in groups of three.

Bidding. Each player in turn must make a bid or pass. Bids are expressed in terms of points in multiples of ten.

*Pinochle is a complex game
that requires practice and strategy.
Good player is hard to beat,
poor one is a cinch. Most popular
form is auction pinochle, played
with 48 cards by three or four people.*

The first player must bid at least 300. Each subsequent bid must be higher than the preceding one. Once a player has passed he may not bid. As soon as two players have passed, the bidding ends with the player who made the highest bid being designated as the "bidder." The other two players now join forces to prevent the bidder from making his contract.

The Widow. If the contract is 300, the bidder may choose to throw in his hand without examining the widow, in which case he must only pay the kitty. With any higher bid, the bidder must expose the widow to all the players and then add it to his hand. At this point the bidder may claim the hand as the obvious winner with his melds, concede (go "bete"), or opt to play out his hand.

Melding. Only the bidder may meld. This is done by displaying meld combinations before beginning the play of the hand. Melds score as follows:

A-K-Q-J-10 in the trump suit (flush): 150 points.
Nine of trumps (dix): 10 points.
K-Q of trumps (royal marriage): 40 points.
K-Q of the same suit other than trump (marriage): 20 points.
Four aces of four different suits (100 aces): 100 points.
Four kings of four different suits (80 kings): 80 points.
Four queens of four different suits (60 queens): 60 points.
Four jacks of four different suits (40 jacks): 40 points.
Queen of spades and jack of diamonds (pinochle): 40 points.

The same card may be counted as part of more than one meld. (However, a card melded in a flush may not be used to meld a royal marriage.)

Value of Cards. Although simpler-value counts are employed in some circles, the count used by all expert players is as follows: 11 points for each ace, 10 points for each ten, 4 points for each king, 3 points for each queen, 2 points for each jack, no points for nines. In addition, 10 points are awarded to the player taking the last trick. Thus, the total number of points available from play is 250.

Burying. After melding, the bidder collects all his cards and places aside face down any three cards that were not employed in melding. At the end of the hand, these three cards will be counted as part of the bidder's score.

The Play. With each player now holding 15 cards, the hands are played. The bidder announces the trump suit and leads the first trick. Each player must, when able, follow suit on each trick. If void in that suit he must play a trump if he can. Otherwise he may play any card. If a trump is led, each player must, if possible, "play over"; that is, play a higher trump than any previously played to that trick. Any trick containing a trump is won by the highest trump played. Any other trick is won by the highest card of the suit led. If two identical cards are played in a trick, the first one played is considered higher. The winner of the previous trick leads to the next.

Scoring. The standard payoffs for a successful bid are as follows: one unit for 300, two units for 350, four units for 400, eight units for 450. For each additional 50 points above 450 the payoff is doubled. (Different payoff schedules are used in some games.) Payoffs are doubled if the trump suit is spades. If the bidder concedes, he must pay the above amount to each of the other players. If he plays out his hand and fails to make the contract ("double bete") he must pay off double to each player.

The Kitty. The kitty is, in effect, a score maintained as if for an imaginary player. It is payed and pays off as do the other players and at the end of the game is divided equally among all players.

Advice on Strategy

The game of pinochle offers a great deal of room for skillful play. Unfortunately, too many players base their play on emotion and intuition—with predictable results—rather than using proper elements of strategy in the game. The following suggestions can significantly strengthen the average player's game:

What to Expect from the Widow. One of the most common errors among auction pinochle players is the tendency to bid high in the hopes that the widow will bail the player out. Mathematical analysis shows that a player who looks to the widow to help him make his melds is being overly optimistic. One can expect the widow to provide playing strength of 20 to 30 points, but not melds. There is the rule: look to the widow for playing strength, *not for melds*. The only exception is the rare hand with three or four places open. In such a situation the player might well bid a hand a little more boldly in a competitive situation in hopes of filling a meld.

Bid Conservatively. The strength of a hand at pinochle can be estimated with considerable precision. Why then do so many players continually make bids they cannot reasonably hope to make? No matter how strong the cards are in your favor, you are going to end up in the hole if you keep having to go bete because you make impossible bids. One reason for this kind of overbidding has already been discussed. Another reason is the tendency to get caught up in competitive bidding until one is in over his head. The situation can be compared to when a person gets so carried away by the bidding at an antique auction that he or she ends up paying much more for an item than intended. The solution is the same in both cases. Set a mental limit on your bid at the outset based on what you can realistically hope to make—and don't allow yourself to go beyond it.

Know Your Opponents. Throughout the game you should be evaluating the playing abilities, tendencies, and bidding practices of your opponents. This knowledge is important in deciding whether to play a questionable hand. If the other players are stronger than you in the play of the cards, concede the hand. The situation is different if you are the strongest player in the game.

Similarly, in competitive bidding it is important to know whether a player can be bid beyond his safe limit. This can only be determined by studying his play throughout the game.

Count Tricks as They are Won. The goal of the bidder is *not* to win the most points possible, but to make his contract. That means that he must keep track of the cards throughout the play of the hand in order to know how close he is to that goal at any given moment and what strategy is most likely to lead to that goal. Too many players fail to do this, figuring that all they have to do is go after every point they can. This can lead to trouble, particularly near the end of the hand. They will often make a risky play in the hopes of grabbing a large number of points, when a far safer play would have won fewer points but enough to make the contract. Don't be greedy, be smart.

3. Dice Games

Dice: small hard cubes, solid squares marked with numbers and used in games of chance. Where do they come from? No one knows. How long have they been used? Forever. What was their original purpose? We can only guess.

History of Dice

Almost every early civilization used some form of dice. Thousands of years before the advent of the white man, American Indians cast dice made of beaver teeth and apricot pits. Beans also were employed, especially by the Aztecs, who practiced a special game called Patoliztli. "Sometimes Montezuma looked on as they played at Patoliztli," writes Lopez de Gomara, "which must resemble the game of tables and which is played with beans marked like one-faced dice which they shake between both hands and throw on a mat."

In Egypt dice have been unearthed from tombs more than two thousand years old, and these are so similar to the ones we know today that if rolled on a layout at Reno hardly anyone would notice. In the British Museum, among the possessions of Queen Hatasu, ruler of Egypt around 1600 B.C., there is a draughts board, twenty lion-headed gaming pieces, and a set of carved dice. The Queen's dice were called "astragals" and were made from the ankle bones of sheep or antelopes. Though they were later used for gaming purposes, their original purpose, we know, was a religious one, serving the temple priests to cast lots and to determine the will of the gods.

By the time the Romans secured some of the action, the function of the dice was purely secular. The Romans named these little squares *alsae* and carved them out of knuckle bones, both human and animal. There were two types of *alsae*: one was four-sided, one was six-sided. They were simultaneously tossed from a box fashioned in the shape of a war tower. The highest throw was called the "throw of the king," the lowest "the throw of the dog." Versions of this roll were played with great frenzy by the Romans and many were the fates decided by such play. It was not by accident that when crossing the Rubicon, Julius Caesar announced that the die had been cast. "When was the madness of games of chance more furious?" asked the poet Juvenal at the height of the Roman gambling craze. "Nowadays not content with carrying his purse to the gaming table, the gamester conveys his iron chest to the playroom. It is there, as soon as the gaming instruments are distributed, you witness the most terrible contests. Is it not mere madness to lose one hundred thousand, and then refuse a garment to a slave who is dying before your eyes from the cold?"

In medieval Europe dicing was strictly forbidden, though we do get occasional glimpses of it through the chinks of the monastery walls. An eleventh-century observer tells us that "clergymen and bishops are fond of dice playing," and a contemporary scholar calls it "the damnable art." In 1190 a decree was passed prohibiting any person in the army beneath the rank of knight to play for money. Knights and clergymen, yes, they could play, but only for twenty shillings a game and just for an hour a day. Those who disobeyed were whipped.

During the reign of Elizabeth I dicing was rife, but the stigma of the white cubes had not yet disappeared. A seventeenth-century account of a unique dice match expresses this contemporary sentiment: "But for a further questionable account of the mischiefs that arise from gaming, this is a very remarkable, but dreadful passage which I shall relate. Near Bellizona in Switzerland three men were playing dice on the Sabbath Day; and one of them called Ulrick Schroeteus, having lost his money, and at last, expecting a good cast, broke out into a most

blasphemous speech, threatening that if fortune deceived him then, he would thrust his dagger into the very body of God, as far as he could. The cast miscarrying, the villain drew his dagger, and threw it against heaven with all his strength; when, behold, the dagger vanished and several drops of blood fell upon the table in the midst of them. And the devil immediately came and carry'd away the blasphemous wretch with such a noise and stink, that the whole city was amaz'd by it. The others, half distracted with fear, strove to wipe out the drops of blood that were upon the table, but the more they rubbed them the more plainly they appear'd. The rumor hereof flying to the city, multitudes of people flocked to the place where they found the gamesters washing the board; whom they bound in chains, and carried towards the prison; but as they were upon the way, one of them was suddenly struck dead, with such a number of lice crawling out of him, as was wonderful and loathsome to behold; and the third was immediately put to death by the citizens to avert the divine indignation."

Despite such "proofs" of divine retribution against the gambler, play in dice continued to flourish.

Hazard was by far the most popular dice game and remained so for several centuries. But in the nineteenth century the American gaming urge inspired a new amusement that was to catapult the humble cubes to new heights of recognition.

The name of the game was craps.

Craps

Craps, the kingpin casino lure. The action in this game is fast, lightning fast. Bets of all sorts can be made on every roll, no waiting. It is the kind of sport in which a gambler can turn up his sleeves and literally jump in. Unlike other casino amusements, where the croupier does all the work, the crap shooter is in the center of things, fingering the action, spieling his monologue, basking in the attention of a dozen or so other dice enthusiasts who are caught up in the drama with him.

Craps is popular for another reason, too. If played properly, it is a relatively fair game, fair enough to give the player—the good player, that is—a chance to win. This chapter is about how to win at the game of craps.

Although a latecomer to the gambler's table, craps boasts an ancient and eminent past. Keeping definitions broad, it can be said that a certain cousin of craps, called *ten*, was popular as far back as Roman times. (It is believed that *ten* was the game Roman soldiers played at the foot of the cross when dicing for the robe of Christ.) Just exactly how *ten* later became the English game of hazard is an open question. But the subsequent mechanics of hazard's evolution into craps is easy to trace, for the similarity between the two games is more than evident.

Observe: the rules for hazard play are simple, simpler by far than craps. Players gather around a circular table presided over by a croupier. The gambler places his bet, allows others to risk an equal amount, and tosses the dice. As he tosses he "calls a main," any number between 5 and 9 inclusive. If he throws that number he "nicks" and wins. If he throws "crabs," a 2 or 3, he loses. And if neither appears the number that does show up becomes his "chance." The object then is to throw his chance before his main. Although rarely played today (the Las Vegas game called hazard is really a version of chuck-a-luck), hazard was at one time the most popular dice game in the world.

Most authorities believe that hazard came to America with the Pilgrims, moved slowly southward, and was finally transformed into craps along the Mississippi by Negro dock workers. That hazard came to America through the French is a theory interesting for its philological lore if not for its factualness. Those propounding this notion believe that around 1800 the game was introduced by French sharpshooters in New Orleans, where after rapidly evolving into modern craps it was dubbed *crapaud*, or "frogeater," by southern locals, who had the habit of referring to all Frenchmen with this quaint sobriquet. Through innumerable slips of the southern tongue, *crapaud* began to sound like *crapoo*, then *crapa*, and finally just plain *craps*: a nice theory, but it is ruined by the fact that gamblers were playing hazard in America some fifty years before the French settled in Louisiana. And anyway, we know exactly where the word "craps" came from. It is a mispronunciation of "crabs," which in hazard indicates a throw of 2 or 3.

It might be said that craps is really two games in one, a schizophrenic package in which one half of the action has little to do with the other. By this we mean that craps, being a game of skill only so far as the betting goes, has two completely different kinds of wagers: those that can and often do win, and those that might but usually do not win. The first kind of wager is made by smart bettors, the second kind by dumb bettors.

Good players, quite simply, play only "line" and "come" bets, plus the odds. (For beginners these and other terms will be explained shortly.) That's it. That's all. Nothing else. On the other hand, dumb bettors waste their money on such flings as the Field, Big 6 and 8, proposition bets, and all the rest. These belong to the dumb game, to the people who are looking for thrills and don't care how they spend their money—those who basically do not care whether they win or lose.

How can one make such a sharp distinction? Look at the statistics. Here, for instance, is a list of percentages for smart crap bettors:

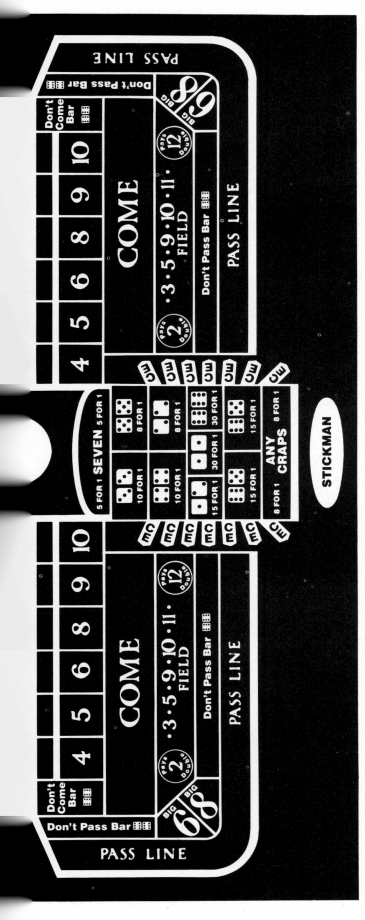

Category One: Smart Craps	
Bet	House Advantage
Pass	1.41%
Don't Pass	1.40%
Come	1.41%
Don't Come	1.40%
Pass line with single odds	0.84%
Don't Pass with double odds	0.59%

Not bad. In fact that 0.59 percent for double odds is about the lowest you will find in the casino, not exactly in favor of the player perhaps, but fair enough to give it a try.

Category Two: Dumb Craps	
Bet	House Advantage
Field	5.26%*
4 or 10 place	6.6%
5 or 9 place	4.0%
Any craps	11.1%
12 or 2 proposition	13.9%
Any 7	16.%
Hard way 4 or 10	11.1%
Hard way 6 or 8	9.%
11 or 3 proposition	11.1%
Big 6 or 8	9.09%

*2.56 when 12 pays triple

You can now see why we speak of dumb craps. Any wagers with such high built-in loss factors as these just can't be very smart. Both kinds of bets nonetheless bear scrutiny.

Smart Craps

To play craps, smart or dumb, the first thing that is required is a casino (unless, of course, you are engaged in a private game, which is something else entirely). Next comes a green felt crap layout, then the dice, then the four house employees (two dealers to place the bets, one boxman to supervise and arbitrate all play, and one stick-man to push and pull the dice and to call the game). Finally, there are the gamblers who may number from one to infinity, as many as the table will accommodate.

The basic game is simple. A shooter starts the action by throwing the dice. This is his "come-out," the first roll of the game. If on the come-out the shooter casts a "natural," a 7 or 11, he immediately wins and a new game begins. If he throws a 2, 3, or 12 he "craps out" and immediately loses. If he throws anything else on the come-out—a 4, 5, 6, 8, 9, or 10—this number becomes his

"point." This means he must continue to roll, trying to make his point before the number 7 turns up. If 7 does appear first, the shooter "sevens-out" and loses the game along with the privilege of throwing the dice. If the point comes up before the 7 he wins. Meanwhile, as the shooter is casting the dice, both he and the other players are making all sorts of bets, not only for or against the shooter's chances of winning, but on the various types of combinations that the dice will be making on each roll. This is the basic game.

Now, if a player wants to play smart craps he must limit himself to four basic bets. The first two of these are known as the line bets: Pass and Don't Pass.

Pass (Front-line) Bet. On the come-out (and only on the come-out), the Pass bettor puts his money in a long section of the layout marked "Win" or "Pass Line." The bettor is wagering that the shooter will win, that he will roll a 7 or 11 on the come-out, or that he will get his point before he sevens-out. In other words, the bettor is wagering on the shooter, making what is called a "right bet." This does not mean the bet is smart or that it is morally commendable, but that it is *with* the shooter rather than against him. If the shooter wins, the Pass bettor collects at even money.

Don't Pass (Back-line) Bet. The player places his money on the "Lose" or "Don't Pass" line, wagering now that the shooter will not throw a 7 or 11 on the come-out or make his point, that he will *lose*. This is called a "wrong bet," the opposite of "right" and against the shooter. Further, the true odds are now somewhat different than in the Pass bet, and consequently on the back-line section of the layout the word "Bar," plus a set of dice showing a 2 or 12 is shown. Here is a bit of self-protection on the part of the casino, which knows that unless the wrong bettor has a standoff, no payoff is made and the Bar 12 or 2 odds would be 1.4 percent in favor of the player! So it "bars" the 12 or 2 on wrong bets, which means that when one of these numbers appears the wrong bettor has a standoff. No payoff is made and the game continues without a stop.

To see these line bets in table play, let's observe an ongoing game of craps. The shooter comes out with a 7 for an immediate win. All Pass bettors collect, all Don't Pass bettors lose, and the shooter comes out again. This time he throws a six. Six becomes his point, and he continues to roll. First he tosses a 5, then another 5. Next comes a 9, then 4, 8, and 10. Finally a 7 shows. He has sevened-out. All Pass bettors lose, all Don't Pass bettors collect. And since the shooter has lost, the dice move clockwise to the player on his left. The new shooter now comes out with a 3. Craps! All Pass bets lose, all Don't Pass bets win.

Come Bet. The third smart craps bet, the Come bet, is an especially dynamic wager for, unlike the Pass bet which is placed only on the come-out, Come bets can be made every time the dice are shaken. This is because the Come bet treats each roll of the dice as the *first roll*, and in this sense is its own separate come-out. To understand this, let's watch a Come bettor at work. The shooter has just come out with a 9. Before the next roll the Come bettor makes a wager. A 4 is now rolled, and this becomes the Come bettor's point. (If the shooter had rolled a 7, the Come bettor would have won, just as on the come-out; and, conversely, if the shooter had rolled craps he would have lost.) From now on the Come bettor needs a 4 before a 7 to win. The original come-out point of 9 does not affect his Come bet in any way. Furthermore, the Come bettor can make another Come bet on the next roll, and then another and another, and so on until the shooter wins or loses. As on the line bets, the payoff is at even money.

Don't Come Bet. A Don't Come bettor wagers that on rolls subsequent to the come-out the shooter will crap out or miss his point. As with the Don't Pass bets, there is a built-in percentage saver here for the casino, a Bar 12 or 2. (As far as the 12 and the 2 go, it really makes no percentage difference which one is barred. In Las Vegas it is usually the 12, in Tahoe and Reno the 2. Certain spots, however, bar the 3 rather than the 12 or 2, and since 3 shows up about twice as often as 2 or 12 it makes good sense to stay away from places like these.) Don't Come, like Come, pays off at even money.

The Odds. These four bets—Pass, Don't Pass, Come, and Don't Come—are unquestionably the most sensible in craps. Yet it is possible to improve these bets. The way to do it is to bet the "odds," the only bets in any casino that give the house almost no edge at all.

For example, suppose you make a ten-dollar Pass bet and the come-out is 6. The house then allows you to bet an amount equal to your original bet (by placing the chips just behind your original bet) that the shooter will win; and if he does, this second bet pays off at *true odds*. True odds means the *actual probabilities* of the dice showing the shooter's point. In the case of a 6 the probability that it will turn up is 6 to 5, so the odds bettor will receive a 6-to-5 payoff on his odds bet. For a point of 5 or 9 the payoff is 3 to 2. For a 4 or 10 it is 2 to 1. For an 8 it is 6 to 5, and so on.

Consequently, odds bets reduce the already low 1.4 percent house edge on Pass and Come bets to literally a fraction of a point. And that's not all. Some houses—this is rare, to be sure—allow the player double odds; he can take or give odds for twice the amount of his original bet, lowering the house advantage even more.

Obviously, all aspiring winners should thoroughly familiarize themselves with the *how*'s and *why*'s of odds betting. The casino never advertises such bets, nor will the croupier ever suggest them; they do not make club owners rich. The only reason they are offered at all is as an enticement to hip crap players who normally would never go near the dice table if the only things it offered were the sucker bets advertised in such bold and brazen letters across the felt.

Pass, Don't Pass, Come, Don't Come, plus the odds, that is the way to bet at craps, the only way—unless of course you have perverse self-destructive urges. Or unless you want to play just for the fun of it. If that is the case, don't go away. You are a candidate for, if you will pardon please the expression, dumb craps.

Dumb Craps
Dumb craps does not always have to be dumb. That is,

it is always a dumb thing to put your dollars on dumb-craps bets. But perhaps you happen to have a walletful tonight, you are feeling p-a-r-t-i-c-u-l-a-r-l-y lucky, and you want to go for broke, as the saying goes. So, proceed. Make some of the chancier bets. Just don't get into the habit. There are, after all, several of these bets that can make you a very rich gambler in a very short time. The first of them is called the proposition bet.

Proposition Bets. In the center of the crap layout is a square box displaying pictures of various dice combinations. Each compartment in the box represents a separate proposition bet. Briefly, they are as follows:

Hard-way Bets. The player bets that a particular number will be rolled the "hard" way, i.e., with doubles, before it is made the statistically more common way, or before a 7 appears. For example, hard-way 4 is rolled with a 2 plus 2. The easy way is 3 plus 1. Hard-way 6 is 3 plus 3. Easy ways are 4 plus 2 and 5 plus 1. The odds against hard-way numbers are high, and payoffs are scarcely commensurate with risk. The odds on hard-way 4 and 10 are 8 to 1, with the house paying 7 to 1, an 11 percent advantage. The odds on 6 and 8 are 10 to 1 with the house paying 9 to 1, a 9.1 percent advantage. Advice: Stay away. This is one of the poorest bets in craps.

Any Seven. The worst! This bet is that a 7 will appear on the next turn of the dice. The payoff is 4 to 1, which makes the house bite a horrifying 16.7 percent, almost as bad as some of the slots! For Super-Suckers only.

Any Craps. The bet is that the next roll will be craps. It is a one-roll bet, like Any Seven, and like Any Seven, the odds are miserable.

Double Six. The bettor wagers that the dice will show boxcars, i.e., two 6s. Pays off at a staggering 30 to 1, but the true odds are 35 to 1, giving the house a 13.9 percent edge.

Double Ace. Same principle as Double Six, same odds, and same house percentage. The bet is that snake eyes, i.e., two 1s, will be rolled.

Eleven. The bet here is that 11 will show on the dice. Players get 15 to 1, or 15 *for* 1. The true odds are 17 to 1. The house edge is 11.9 percent.

Three. The bet is that a 3 will appear on the next roll. The odds are 15 to 1, or 15 *for* 1. The true odds and house advantage are the same for Eleven. Note: The words "to" and "for" as in "15 to 1" and "15 for 1" are definitely *not* interchangeable. "To" means that the gambler will win the payoff money *plus* get his original bet back. "For" indicates that the gambler wins *only* the payoff and *does not* get his original bet returned. Thus if a casino offers a payoff at 16 for 1, it is just a tricky way of saying 15 to 1.

Big 6 or 8. Another conspicuous section of the crap layout advertises Big 6 and Big 8. The player bets that either an 8 or a 6, whichever one he has his money on, will turn up before a 7. To make this bet is simply silly, mathematically speaking, for statistically 7 appears more frequently than 6 or 8, or any other number, for that matter.

The Field. Printed above the Don't Pass section of the layout is a long strip of numbers reading 2,3,4,9,10,11, 12, with the word "Field" below. The player bets that one of the numbers listed, any one at all, will appear on the next roll. For example, if a 2,3,4,9,10,11, or 12 appears on the next roll the bettor wins, and conversely, if it is 5,6,7,8, or 9 he loses. Though the Field payoff is at even money, the casino usually gives double for a 2 or 12 as added inducement, and in some casinos a 5 is substituted for a 4, also improving the odds. It all seems a pretty good deal, but it isn't. Though there are more winning field numbers than losing ones, the losing numbers show up with far greater frequency than the winning ones, cancelling out any advantage the added enticements provide. It is worth noting, however, that in some houses 12 and 2 pay triple, lowering the house advantage to 2.5 percent. In this case the Field becomes one of the few respectable wagers in the dumb craps category. Most experienced players generally regard field bets as poor risks, however.

Box-number Bets. The top of the crap layout displays a banner of numbers reading "4, 5, six, 8, nine, and 10." A player can "buy" one of these numbers by paying the casino a commission charge of 5 percent of the total wager. If this number then appears he collects a true-odds payoff at the following schedule: for a 4 or 10, 2 to 1; for a 5 or 9, 3 to 2; for a 6 or 8, 6 to 5. The house advantage in each case is 4.76 percent which is the way it works out after the commission is figured into the bet.

Place-number Bets. To make a box-number bet and pay commission is known as "buying a number." Another way to bet the 4, 5, six, 8, nine, and 10 is to "place" them. When this is done the gambler pays no commission, but neither does he receive his payoff at anything approaching true odds. In place betting the payoff odds are as listed:

Numbers	Payoff	House Advantage
4 and 10	9 to 5	6.66%
5 and 9	7 to 5	4.00%
6 and 8	7 to 6	1.51%

A player can also "lay" a bet, which means that he bets on the numbers to *lose* rather than to win. Such bets are rare, and since the odds are better for placing, they are not worth the effort. Note that the house advantage on the 6 and 8 is a surprising 1.51 percent, making this the one smart bet among a multitude of losers.

Bank craps—the cast: starring the shooter, in foreground; with two dealers, standing on right in white shirts; boxman, sitting between two dealers; stickman, center left.

*Spots before your eyes. Dealer
collects and pays off bets with blurring
speed. Bottom left: When a die
is leaning against something—backboard,
chips, another die—it's called
a "cocked die," and the face up counts.*

The Odds at a Glance

No player should enter a game before he knows what his chances are, mathematically speaking. This is the first law of good gambling. So here for perusal, study, and—for the ambitious—memorization, are the odds at a number of the most popular gambling games.

A Few Suggestions

These are the bare facts of good and bad craps playing. Stick with the smart bets and you have a decent chance of winning. Go with the bad and you will probably lose. Whichever way you intend to go, however, here are a few suggestions:

If you are a beginner, don't jump in whole hog right away. Craps is, after all, a complicated affair. Get clear on basic betting procedure first. Start with the Pass line and learn it thoroughly. (Watching others bet often is helpful.) Then move on to the Don't Pass bet, and after you are comfortable with these two, bet the Come and Don't Come bets. Only after you are familiar with these, thoroughly familiar, should you start betting the odds. Also, in the beginning make one bet at a time. It is hard to keep track of a number of wagers and you can't expect the dealer to do it for you. He probably will, but if he doesn't it's your fault, not his. Start slowly, learn the rules, the system, the odds, and build from there.

Familiarize yourself with the percentages before you play craps. This means not only the odds on each bet, but also the probabilities of rolling each number on the dice. A reiteration: the worst bets in craps are the one-

Odds Against Throwing a Particular Number on the Dice						No. of Combinations	Chances
Roll	Ways It Can Be Shown on Dice						
2	1-1					1	1 in 36
3	1-2	2-1				2	2 in 36
4	1-3	3-1	2-2			3	3 in 36
5	1-4	2-3	3-2	4-1		4	4 in 36
6	1-5	2-4	3-3	4-2	5-1	5	5 in 36
7	1-6	2-5	3-4	4-3	5-2 6-1	6	6 in 36
8	2-6	3-5	4-4	5-3	6-2	5	5 in 36
9	3-6	4-5	5-4	6-3		4	4 in 36
10	4-6	5-5	6-4			3	3 in 36
11	5-5	6-5				2	2 in 36
12	6-6					1	1 in 36

*Dealer racks up the
winnings. Sometimes silver
dollars are used instead
of $1 chips. Dice buck or marker
in lower left is used
to identify shooter's point.*

Odds on Different Bets in Craps		
Bet	Payoff Odds	Casino Advantage
Pass line	1–1	1.41%
Don't pass	1–1	1.40%
Come	1–1	1.41%
Don't come	1–1	1.40%
Field (2,3,4, 9,10,11,12)	1–1	11.11%
Field (2,3,4,9,10,11,12. Double on 2 or 12)	1–1	5.26%
Field (2,3,5,9, 10,11,12)	1–1	5.55%
Big 6	1–1	9.09%
Big 8	1–1	9.09%
Hard way 4 or 10	7–1	11.11%
Hard way 6 or 8	9–1	9.09%
Any craps	7–1	11.11%
11 or 3 proposition	15–1	16.66%
12 or 2 proposition	30–1	16.66%
Any 7	4–1	16.66%
Pass line with single odds	1–1 plus odds	.84%
Pass line with double odds	1–1 plus odds	.60%
Don't pass with single odds	1–1 plus odds	.83%
Don't pass with double odds	1–1 plus odds	.59%

roll action bets. Next come Any Craps, Eleven, Any Seven, etc. Then come the Hard-way bets, then Big 6 and 8 and the Field, then the box numbers, and finally the place numbers. The best are the Pass and Come bets placed with odds. So learn and win by knowing the odds and percentages in the table shown here.

The crap table can be a sense-stimulating place with many economic and social distractions to erode one's common sense. So be careful. Decide beforehand how much you can afford to lose and then stick to this decision no matter *how* persuasive the stickman's urgings or *how* enticing the odds. Don't get suckered into sucker bets in the heat of the moment. You will regret them in the cold of the following day.

A Short Dictionary of Dice

Ace. *On the dice, the number 1.*

African dominoes. *Slang for dice.*

Bank craps. *Casino crap game.*

Banker. *Someone who finances a dice game.*

Big dick. *On the dice, the number 10.*

Blanket roll. *A cheating maneuver made during the dice roll, possible only on a soft surface like a blanket.*

Bounce shot. *A cheating maneuver made during the dice roll, where the dice are made to fall practically dead without rolling.*

Busters. *Mis-spotted dice (q.v.).*

Boxcars. *On the dice, the number 12 made by two 6s.*

Bust-out man. *A dice cheat who specializes in switching "stops" in and out of a game.*

Calipers. *Dice that are true to 1/1000 of an inch.*

Capped dice. *Fixed dice on which certain sides are made more resilient than others, so that certain numbers are more likely to appear.*

Come out. *The crap shooter's first roll of the dice.*

Deuce. *On the dice, the number 2.*

Doorpops. *Mis-spotted dice that make 7 or 11 only.*

Eighter from Decatur. *On the dice, the number 8.*

Fade. *Accept a bet in craps.*

Fader. *A bettor who covers part or all of a shooter's bet in private craps.*

Flat. *Fixed dice that have been shaved down to irregular shapes and that favor certain sides.*

Galloping dominoes. *Slang for dice.*

Hot. *Describes the crap shooter during a lucky streak.*

Ice. *Protection money paid off during a dice game.*

Juice-joint. *A dishonest casino, where the dice are electronically controlled.*

Levels. *Honest dice.*

Little Joe. *Point 4 in dice.*

Load. *A weight inserted into the dice which makes them favor certain sides.*

Loads. *Loaded dice (q.v. load).*

Memphis dominoes. *Slang for dice.*

Misses (or Missouts). *Fixed dice designed to make more 7s than passes.*

Mis-spots. *Fixed dice on which certain numbers are repeated.*

Natural eight. *Two 4's in craps.*

No dice. *A mis-roll. A roll that is not allowed during a game.*

Off number. *Any number on the dice except what the shooter is trying to make.*

Palm holdout. *A cheating maneuver whereby extra dice are kept palmed.*

Passe-dix. *French dice game.*

Rats. *Slang for dice.*

Ring in. *To secretly introduce crooked dice into a game.*

Shapes. *Fixed dice that have been altered in shape so that they are not true cubes and so that they favor certain numbers.*

Side bet. *Bet made between craps players or onlookers on outcome of the roll.*

Six-ace flats. *Fixed dice whose 6 and 1 sides have a larger area than all other sides which are thus favored during the roll.*

Snake eyes. *When the total of both dice is 2.*

Tops. *Fixed dice on which certain numbers are repeated.*

Trey. *On the dice, the number 3.*

Two-bit craps. *Small stakes.*

Work. *Crooked dice.*

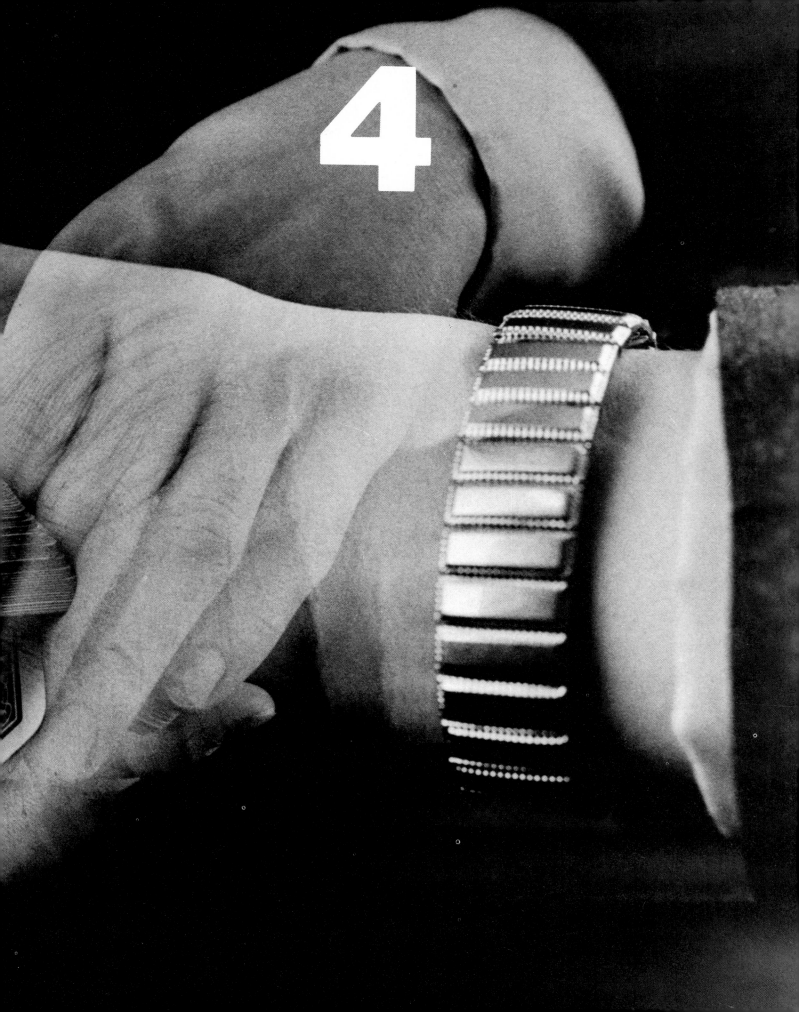

4. On Your Guard: Cheating

More cheating goes on in private games of "fun" than in any other kind of gambling. Yes, there is more cheating in the private game than in the clip joints, at the rigged wheels, or anywhere else. Why? Because people don't usually expect such things from their friends. And because it's easy to fool others when they're not expecting it—and because it's so tempting.

This is not to make you paranoid. *Most* games are straight. And those that aren't straight are worth learning about because if you participate in private games of gambling, chances are that someday someone will try to cheat you.

Cheating at Cards

Anyone who has ever seen a master card mechanic knows just what utterly astonishing magic he can do. The layman simply doesn't believe it: the sharp deals out a royal flush at will, stacks a deck while he shuffles, and is in total control of everything that goes on under your nose without your being aware of it. In the pictures that follow, gambling expert Darwin Ortiz, considered by many to be the finest card manipulator in the country and a leading expert on card cheating methods, demonstrates some standard dirty tricks. Unlike most card mechanics who specialize in one or two cheating techniques, Darwin can indetectably execute all of them. He does a few of the most popular moves for us here.

In picture sequence A, the standard top deal is illustrated. Although there is no cheating maneuver going on here, notice that the dealer is holding the deck in the "mechanic's grip," a tipoff for what is to come.

In picture sequence B, the dealer is still holding the cards in the mechanic's grip, with the thumb extended diagonally almost to the opposite corner of the deck and the other fingers curled around and under. The

forefinger is curled around the outer right-hand corner. The mechanic's grip is a pretty good indication of funny business. Here, the dealer is executing the "second deal," dealing the second card from the top. He starts to push the top card off the deck. The left thumb comes over as if to take it, but instead contacts the exposed corner of the second card and deals it out while the right thumb simultaneously retracts the top card square with the deck. In these pictures (as in all others here) the move is slowed and exaggerated for clarity. When skillfully executed, it is almost impossible for a layman to detect. Second dealing is one of the most popular methods of cheating at cards.

The so-called "bottom deal" is shown in picture sequence C. Again, the mechanic's grip is used. The dealer knows beforehand which card is on the bottom of the deck. He appears as if he were dealing the first card, but at the same instant pulls off the bottom card. His opposite thumb then pushes the top card rapidly back in place.

There are many varieties of false shuffles as well as false deals. Observe the "push-through" maneuver shown in picture sequence D. The shuffler apparently shuffles fair and square but in fact he has not really mixed the cards at all. The deck is divided in half and the corners are legitimately woven together. Note that the halves, however, are never completely squared. The two separate packets are pushed into each other at an angle so that the two halves can be independently controlled, each hand controlling its half. The shuffler concludes by stripping out one half and placing it under the other, simulating a cut. When properly done, it is impossible to distinguish this stripout action from a legitimate cut.

For the expert it takes but little maneuvering to palm a card—a card will fit into the human hand without

Text continued on page 134

A Standard deal

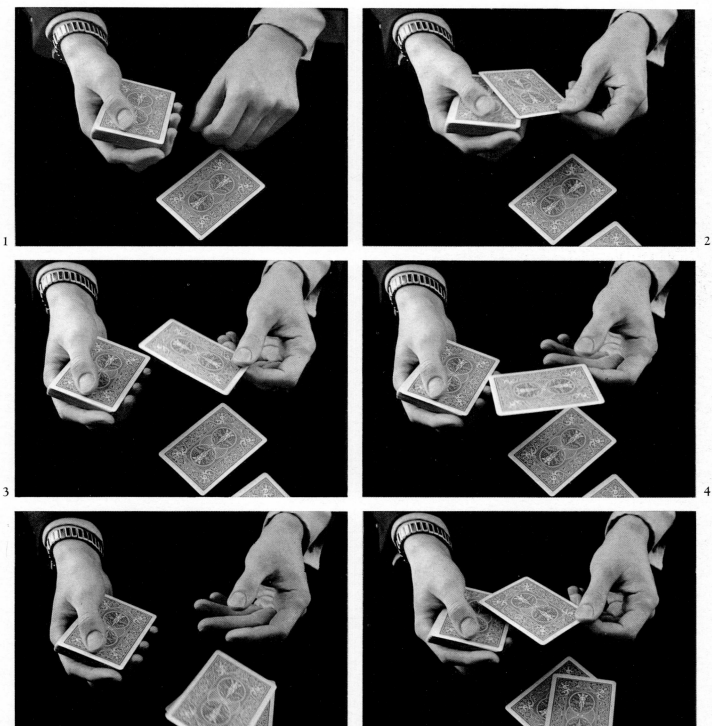

Second and bottom dealing are
commonly used cheating methods at
blackjack, among other games.
In B, dealer knows there is a desirable
card on top of deck that would
go to another player. He
uses this maneuver to hold
back card for himself.

1

2

3

B Second deal

1

2

3

C Bottom deal

1

2

3

1

2

3

7

D **Push-through**

5

4

4

5

5

6

8

Using push-through maneuver, cheat can keep cards in same order, stacked for him to win. Picture 5 shows what the other players see— apparently conclusion of honest shuffle. Picture 6 is exposed view of what other players never see.

E Palming

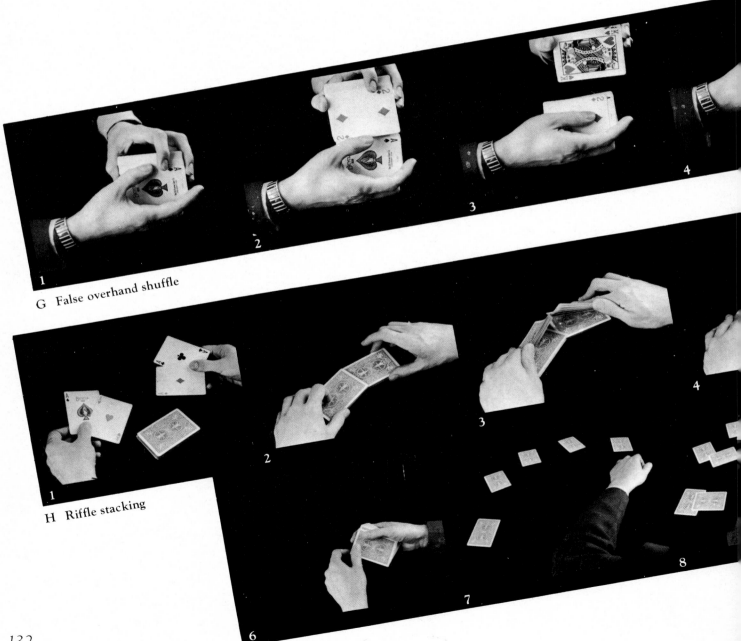

G False overhand shuffle

H Riffle stacking

Palming—a well known cheating
technique—enables cheat to hold
on to the desired card and
add it to his hand. It is not used
as often as people think because
of risk of being caught red-handed.
In G, cards are shown face
up just to illustrate this move.

5

6

7

5

9

10

11

Riffle stacking. Cheat has
previously controlled aces to top
of deck (picture 1). He
apparently shuffles honestly (2),
but through sense of touch (3, 4, 5)
he controls the order that cards
interlace, positioning aces to fall where
he wants. Cards are now
dealt fair and square (6-11),
showing that aces have been
maneuvered to desired positions.

a trace. In picture sequence E we see a mechanic "holding out" a card. Then, using the same basic palming maneuver in picture sequence F, the dealer steals the card off the bottom of the deck.

Another cheating maneuver, called the "false overhand shuffle," is shown in picture sequence G. The shuffler knows where he wants the ace of spades to end up, and after a bit of what appears to be legitimate mixing he lands it where it began.

Probably the most difficult sleight-of-hand cheating method to master is "riffle stacking," as demonstrated in picture sequence H. It is also the most worthwhile to know because it is the safest form of cheating. When executed on an expert level, there are no visual tipoffs, even to another expert. After manipulating the cards through sense of touch, stacking them in the desired order, the dealer ends up with what appears to be a fully shuffled deck. He can then deal himself four aces. A good card man can maneuver the deck while he's shuffling, while he's cutting, and while he's dealing.

Dice and Other Accouterments

Dice mechanics can do things that are equally as flashy as the stunts of the card sharks. Even with the dice hustler's most basic move, the so-called "lock grip" shown in picture I, enormous control can be exerted over the roll. The dice are held firmly in the crease of the two middle fingers with the thumb locked up tight behind. The gambler pretends to shake the dice but really just knocks them together while holding them in place. Then he lets them go in this exact position. Chances are good they will come up in his favor.

Many crooked gamblers don't bother to learn such techniques, it should be said. Why bother when there are so many species of gaffed dice on the market and when most rubes can't tell the difference? All one has to learn is how to switch the dice, that is, switch out the good ones and switch in the phonies. The elite dice cheat does this by concealing an extra pair of dice, the gaffed ones, in the palm of his hand as in picture J. When it's his turn he exchanges one pair of dice for another through some nimble fingerwork, passing the palmed articles up to the fingers and the good dice back to the palm, all without a telltale click or rattle. Later he retrieves the crooked dice in a similar manner.

Less accomplished cheats will pull the "money switch." One set of dice is substituted for another under a batch of dollar bills held in the same hand as the dice. The cheater is simply making a bet, isn't he? In fact he's pulling a switch under the camouflage of the bills. Or the cheater may simply switch the dice when no one is looking, under the table or from hand to hand—a fairly gross procedure perhaps but often effective, especially among greenhorns. Or the cheater may not switch the dice at all, taking his chances that no one in the game will be sophisticated enough to spot the fact that he's been using phony dice the whole time.

And indeed phony dice are not always easy to spot. One must be looking, *and* one must know what to look for. An exemplary pair of crooked dice, a simple and highly accessible set too, are called "doorpops." These can be purchased at any novelty shop or penny arcade and often will be sold under the misleading title of "loaded dice." Their premise is so ridiculously simple it seems laughable at first: one die only has 5s on it; the other has only 6s and 2s, as in picture K. Obviously they'll roll a 7 or 11 each time, handy indeed for the game of craps—for which, incidentally, fake dice are almost exclusively manufactured. Doorpops are so obvious that usually they are brought in and out of a game with a hasty dispatch.

I
J

Doorpops (K), shapes (L), bevels (M), and raised-edge dice (N)—all varieties of crooked dice are used on the unsuspecting chump. The mechanic will usually not operate in big casinos but in floating crap games and the like.

K

L

Less apparent are "shapes" (L), sometimes called "bricks" or "flats." These are dice from which a tenth to a thirtieth of an inch has been shaved off one of the sides so that the finished cube, upon inspection, is slightly rectangular, not exactly square. On one variety of brick, the so-called "6-ace flat," the shaving is removed from the side with the 6 or 1. This leaves more surface area on the shaved side (the other sides are slightly truncated now and have less surface exposed) so that the dice will land on 6 or 1 with greater frequency. Such dice tend to further crap (1-1 or 6-6) or seven (6-1 or 1-6), and are called "missouts." Missouts are for the "wrong" bettors, those who are wagering against the shooter. "Passers," on the other hand, are any dice which favor the shooter, the "right" bettor.

Another variety of gaffed dice, called "bevels," are dice on which a side is slightly bowed or curved, describing a subtle convex hump, as shown in picture M. Whenever the die lands on its curved side it will have a tendency to keep rolling, thus favoring the sides (and the numbers) which are *not* beveled. An easy way to detect bevels is to press one die against the other. If the dice have a tendency to "rock," chances are one side is bowed.

A member in good standing in the arsenal of crooked devices too is the "raised-edge" die, as shown in picture N. Here the name speaks for itself. One edge of the die has been heated and pressed in such a manner that it protrudes slightly, expanding the surface area of that side and increasing the possibility of that side appearing. To detect raised-edge work simply run a finger along the edge of the suspect dice. The sharp, overlapping edge will give its own testimony.

By now it should be clear that except for the most obvious varieties of phony dice like mis-spots, crooked dice are engineered to increase the *possibilities* of rolling

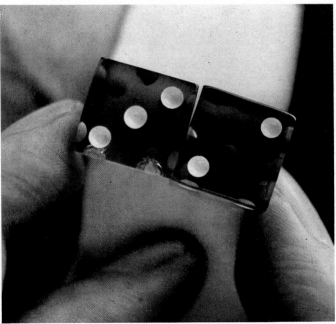

certain numbers and are by no means guaranteed to produce those numbers every time. The reason for this is obvious, as any player who continually tossed the same combination would quickly be suspect. With other kinds of cheating apparatus the same principle abides: such devices are designed to enhance one's chances of winning but by no means to ensure them.

In cards for instance, a rather chancy bit of merchandise is the so-called "shiner," as shown in picture O. This can really be just about any kind of reflecting surface, a finger ring, a sequin, a polished fingernail, though there are actual reflecting surfaces made specifically to fit the contours of the finger which act as little hidden mirrors to read several of the cards and improve one's knowledge of the odds. With these diminutive seeing eyes the dealer can catch quick sight of the card he is giving to a fellow player, can see the bottom card—all kinds of things. Anyone who wears a shiner, however, is taking his life

The cheat may be taking his life in his hands by using a shiner (O). Safer but still obvious is the punch, which makes a blisterlike mark in the cards. Skilled card manipulators, such as Darwin Ortiz (r), do not need such devices to come up with winners.

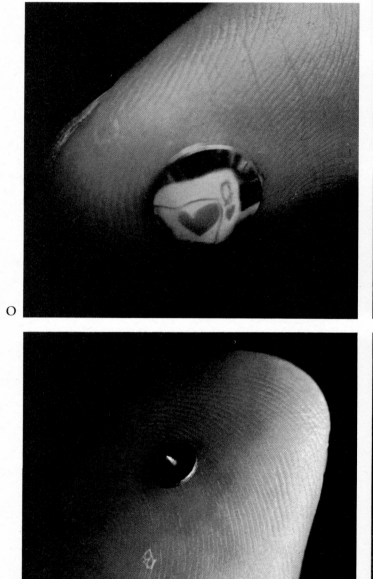

O

P

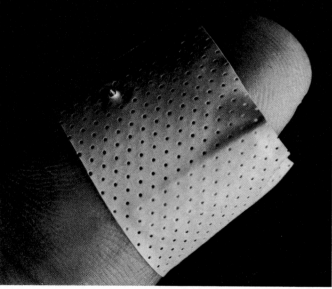

in his hands. As can be seen, it is anything but obscure.

Only slightly less obtrusive is the thumb punch, as shown in picture P. It is a small tacklike object that the cheater adheres to a finger. It makes quaint little puncture marks along the sides of the cards, marking them to the cheater's specifications. Trouble with the thumb punch is that it's hard to keep on one's finger, and as a result most people are reduced to putting it under a bandage. That's why smart card players are always wary of opponents that come into a game with bandages over their "cuts."

For deck marking too there is "daubing," which is demonstrated in picture sequence Q. It is a rather messy but effective means of improving the odds. Unbeknownst to his fellows, the cheater smears a tiny bit of red or blue salve on one of his fingers, then transfers the salve to the back of one of the cards. The salve, of course, is coordinated to blend with the color of the card and the smear becomes a clear but subtle sign to the dauber. Once again, the deck has been subtly marked.

Of course, if one wants to bypass all these digital acrobatics he can simply buy a deck of marked cards. Interestingly, one deck out of every hundred in the United States is marked. And one should not be fooled that such marked decks are obvious or that they are easy to decipher. Some of the most ingenious techniques are used in this field and the results are often unreadable for anyone but the seasoned vet.

In the cards taken from Deck 1, which has been marked with so-called "stem work," note the three main branching stems between the balls with the enclosed birds. Note how in the first card all three stems are unmarked, but in the second card the stem to the right is shortened. In the third, the center stem is shortened, and so on. Each of these marks coincides with a card value; that is, the first card is a 2, the second a 3, etc.

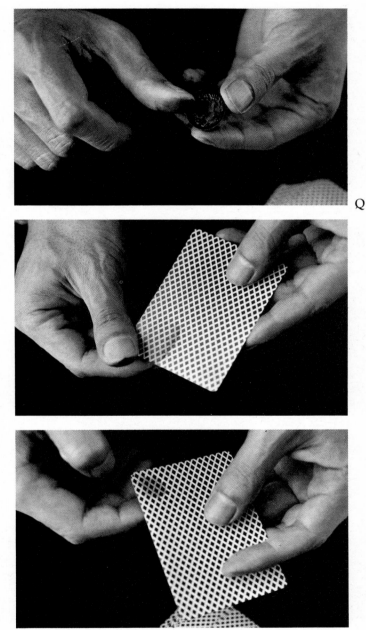

Q

Deck 1

1

2

3

Deck 2

1

2

Deck 3

Be wary of extraordinary runs of bad luck—
you might be playing with a marked deck.
Opposite: There are many ways to mark a deck,
and these are simple but effective methods.
Any professional gambler can detect such markings,
and so can you if you know what to look for.

In Deck 2 the marking is more obvious but still neatly disguised. Note the outer border, the indented boxes with dots in them. In the first card the seventh dot from the right on the top border is "blocked." This card is a 3. In the next card the dot next to it is missing. This card is a 4. Such marks can easily be seen from across a table by anyone who is looking for them.

Deck 3 shows a different technique entirely. This time the marking is not within the pattern on the back of the card, but in the border surrounding it. On the upper lefthand border of the card a slight bulge or blip can be seen opposite the seventh square down. The placement of each blip is coordinated to the number.

Incidentally, a good test for marked cards is to take the deck and fan through it, carefully watching the pattern on the back as you do. If there are markings they will start to "jump," something like the old flip-cards which when riffled through made animated designs. If you notice anything moving in a strange way zero in on it and see if it's been tampered with. Once one marking is found the rest are easy to see.

Interview with a Dice and Card Manufacturer

The following interview was conducted in the offices of a certain Mr. X. We call him Mr. X because he prefers to have his name withheld from publication. Mr. X is an affable old gentleman of, say, seventy, who has been in the business for more than fifty years. From his plant in New York City's garment district he reminisces about his life in the business, the different types of merchandise he produces, and the surprising facts concerning "trick" cards and the "trick" dice industry.

Q *Give me an idea, if you would, of the type of merchandise you manufacture in your shop.*

A Well, before I do that I just want you to realize that everything we manufacture in this place is for magic purposes, exposé purposes, and tricks. We can't ascertain as to what purpose people are going to use the material after they buy it, so we can't guarantee anything. All we know is that we manufacture materials that are predominantly for magic purposes.

Q *When people come in here, are there any restrictions on the type of things they can buy? Can they get it all over the counter?*

A No, there are no restrictions. As long as we have our rules that none of the materials are intended for illegal or gambling purposes it's O.K.

Q *I'm interested in sample prices. What do a pair of loaded dice cost, for instance?*

A Some cost fifty cents, some a dollar a pair. Some will cost five dollars a pair, some ten. It depends on type. There are certain kinds that are perfect dice. They can never go wrong when you use them, you understand me? You see, dice are the backbone of our business, and not just the loaded kind, either. We sell thousands of good dice to the casinos 'cause they know we make the best dice you can get hold of. Those dice you buy in the drugstores or magic stores are imperfect dice. They are not cut properly, and maybe one side is shorter or rougher than another. Our dice are perfect. You see, there are two ways of making dice. To make cheap dice you use cutoff saws for cutting them. The saws are irregular and imperfect, and so are the dice. Then they are drilled with multiple drills and they use a system of spotting them by dipping them in a vat of paint. Perfect dice, on the other hand, have to be hardened and seasoned first. The celluloid we use for our dice has been seasoned three different times till it achieves the proper state where it will not shrink or become distorted because of heat conditions. Climatic conditions mean nothing to perfect dice. Imperfect ones will warp in bad heat. That's why good crap players insist on perfect dice. We do all the second and third stages of cutting and drilling the celluloid here. The dice are cut to 1/10,000 of an inch. Our machines are accurate to that degree. Our maximum tolerance is 1/5 or 1/10,000 of an inch, and that's pretty good. After the dice are cut to this measurement they are then either sanded—Las Vegas likes sanded dice—or they are polished.

Q *Do you allow people to come in here and watch how the dice are made?*

A No, that's my secret.

Q *You mean that the method for manufacturing perfect dice is not common knowledge?*

A That's right.

Q *Could you give me now some idea of the kind of things you manufacture here? Especially the trick stuff?*

A Well, for example, we make mis-spots here. You know mis-spotted dice? By mis-spots I mean that the dice have double numbers on them. If you wanted the dice to make even numbers only, you would mark the dice with two 1s, two 3s, and four 5s. Now, when they are rolled they can only make even numbers. Or with a pair of dice you can take the first die and mark it with 5s on all sides and take the second and mark it with two 6s and four 2s. In other words, you can make nothing but 7 or 11 with them —pretty good if you shoot craps. These are mis-spots. We call them "doorpops" too. How they got that name I wouldn't know. I suppose it came through the years.

Then you have your "shapes," another kind of trick dice. Now, shapes can never be seen by a sucker. They are cut so that the surface of the 6 and 1 are larger than the 2,3,4, and 5. You can't miss them if you look.

Q *What value are they if they can be seen so easily?*

A If someone was going to cheat with them he would switch them into the game for a few rolls and then switch them out. You see, shapes will show the 6 and the 1 percentagewise more times than other numbers. This makes them losing dice which, as you know, is good for certain bets at craps. Maybe you want to avoid a 7. So you use shapes. Remember though, they work on percentage. They are not *likely* to roll a 7. They just might. But they are not likely. The same is true with loaded dice. If you had a set that rolled 7 and 11 *every* time it would be pretty suspicious. So loaded dice are made to show these numbers more often than others. Loaded dice are not a sure thing.

Q *How are loaded dice made?*

A They are made with different types of weight inserted into them. The different metals and amalgams we use make them favor certain numbers more than others.

Q *Do you make them here?*

A We can make them here, yes.

Q *So would it be safe to say that there are basically three kinds of trick dice: mis-spots, shapes, and loaded dice?*

A Yes, that would be correct. There are other kinds, too, but they are rarely used.

Q *Since we're talking about trick devices, what about cards?*

A Well, cards have fallen off lately, you understand? They use cards a lot for magic tricks, that's all. For gambling they're not used very much. This is because in the past years lots of people have learned to use sleight of hand so they don't need marked cards. It's too risky. You can get away with a lot more using sleight than with marked cards.

Q *The markings on some of the decks you have shown me are tiny.*

A They are not all small though. There are small marks and there are large marks. And there are sharp-eyed people who can see the finest kind of work. And there are others who are practically blind. You have to cut out half the design for them to be able to see it.

Q *Are most people in the second category?*

A Well, I wouldn't say that. I would say that most people are in a middle category.

Q *How can you catch someone using marked cards when the markings are so small and subtle?*

A No, you don't understand. I'm telling you, they're not so difficult to see. The only people who don't discover marked cards are those who don't look. If you look for it you'll find it. But I'm telling you, marked cards aren't used much any more. They say that the hand is quicker than the eye, but personally I think that is a fallacy. If you know how to manipulate cards, you know there are ways of *hiding* the hands from the eye, that's all. That's why sleight is becoming so popular. Today one has to watch the hands more than the cards.

Q *Do you make roulette wheels here also?*

A No, sir. Hardly anyone makes roulette wheels today in this country. You see, some years back there was a man named Rosenthal, a casino operator. Rosenthal was paying off the police. But despite this fact the police were still arresting him. This was about sixty years ago. Rosenthal kicked too loud, so the chief of police ordered four men to assassinate him. They were caught. The four assassins and the chief of police were sent to the electric chair. After that scandal the gambling laws were tightened up and lots of people who manufactured gambling equipment went out of business. Roulette wheels were made illegal; to manufacture, that is.

Q *So no one makes the wheels anymore?*

A Not in this country. In fact, I wanted to import roulette wheels from France. But the Attorney General's office refused to allow them to come in. Of course they could be shipped to a state where gambling is legal, or to the islands. But if you send one to New York it will be destroyed.

Q *What about in Las Vegas?*

A In Nevada I *think* they have one individual who manufactures them. The rest are made in France.

Q *Why is it illegal to manufacture roulette wheels and not cards and dice?*

A Dice and cards are used for social amusement, for entertainment, whereas roulette wheels are totally instruments of gambling.

Q *How did you get involved in this business?*

A Well, years ago I shot craps like yourself. This was before the McClellan Law was passed. The McClellan Law made it illegal to transport gambling paraphernalia over state lines. At that time there were many manufacturers of my type of merchandise. There was Hunt in Chicago, there was the K.C. Card Company, Mason and Company, Ted Schaeffer, Joe Traybell in St. Louis. I remember a lot of them. Then when the law was passed lots of these companies went out of business. Now I hadn't been in the business too long when this law was passed. I was hit hard but I managed to get through. I had to stop all shipments over state lines. So now I only sell in New York. But there are plenty of customers here. Plenty.

Yes, I've been in this business a long time, more than fifty-five years. But this business is a dying business. The few companies like ours are cutting each other's throats to get by.

Q *Why is it a dying business?*

A It isn't a large enough commodity to make it worthwhile. How many dice can you sell? How many cards can you sell? Not many. So when a business like mine loses its founders that's usually the end. The business closes down and soon that business is completely forgotten. That's the way it seems to be going, as far as I can tell.

5. The Horses

We love to risk our money on animals that run. Why? Perhaps it is the vicarious spirit of the chase, the instinct to seek and destroy sublimated into a spectator sport. And perhaps also it is the sheer thrill of watching fluid animal movement while—presumably—making a profit out of the whole thing.

Horse Racing from the Beginning

Paleontologists agree that the earliest horse specimen, Perissodactyl, or as he is more familiarly known to us all, the odd-toed ungulate, appeared sometime in the lower Eocene epoch forty to sixty million years ago. He must have been a peculiar-looking creature, this early horse, not only because his neck was short and his muzzle pug-nosed, but because he stood scarcely higher than a cat. The first of his kind was known as Eohippus. Eohippus gave place on the evolutionary ladder to the Meohippus, who slowly became the Hypohippus, who bowed to the Merychippus, and so on in size and intelligence up to our one-toed grazer friend, Equus.

It was around six thousand years ago, according to most estimates, that the first rider saddled the first horse. In the British Museum a carved cuneiform cylinder displays a horse-drawn chariot, and this dates to at least four millennia before Christ. In 2300 B.C., Egyptians already were holding horse races complete with grandstands, jockeys, and purses. Not too many centuries after this the Arabs, who would one day be among the greatest of all horsemen, began breeding the spirit of speed into their mounts by employing the "necessity principle." They would saddle the horses, deprive them of water till the creatures almost dropped from thirst, then give them full reign to romp toward the nearest water hole.

A short time after the horse's domestication its domesticators realized that not only was this creature a dandy vehicle for riding to town, but was, without doubt, the greatest weapon of war since the stone. Ancient peoples were swiftly beaten down by adversaries clever enough and patient enough to cultivate an equestrian war force of charioteers or cavalrymen. The horse changed the balance of power in the ancient world and every nation eventually began breeding them. Courage, stamina, size, all were necessary characteristics for a good fighting steed and, at the same time, all were necessary for a good race horse as well. A horse that could race well could usually fight well, too, and vice versa. Thus the history of horse racing parallels the history of war.

Horse racing first comes to literature in Book Twenty-three of *The Iliad.* Homer tells of a chariot race in which the prize was "a woman skilled in woman's work and a tripod of two and twenty measures with handles on it." Quick to imitate anything Greek, the Romans soon instituted the sport but, as was their way, they turned it into popular spectacle, erecting colossal tracks, like the Circus Maximus, where some 350,000 Romans would crowd in to watch the Ben-Hurs of their day. In such places it was not uncommon to see racing chariots drawn by twenty horses or, on occasion, by dogs and even ostriches.

In Europe the first public races were run during the eleventh century, just outside London. Here horse fairs were held every Friday and here earls and barons mingled with hoi polloi. The nobility came to admire the horse-flesh on display and perchance to purchase some if it ran well that day on the open field. By the end of the eleventh century, horse racing already was a sport of kings. Richard I won forty English pounds of "ready gold" in one of the earliest recorded payoffs at a European track. John, his successor, was the first among royalty to maintain a racing stable and the first to institutionalize the annual three-day race at Chester, where the prize was "a wooden ball, highly valued." In the next few years this prize underwent a number of transformations, becoming a silver ball, then a silver goblet, and finally a silver cup; hence, our custom of awarding a loving cup to the winner of a sporting event.

A certain sheriff at Chester also had a useful notion concerning prizes. After deciding that the silver cup ordered that year for the races was inferior, and after sending the second one back to the silversmith for similar reasons, he found that when he finally got a product he approved of he was faced with the problem of what to do with the first two cups. After thinking this one over for a while, he finally hit upon an idea: Why not award *three* prizes? Give one for first place, one for second, and one for third. Thus evolved win, place, and show.

With the coming to power of the Stuart dynasty in seventeenth-century England, the rise of the races really began. James I, an aficionado of fleet-footed steeds since childhood, built the first real track at Newmarket and put up a handsome building nearby called the King's House, a small but elegant *palazzo* for His Majesty's after-race recreation. At Newmarket a spectators' stand was erected, races run, and for a time horses were the thing. The next monarch, Charles I, unfortunately put something of a damper on riding activity by simply ignoring it. The Puritan Cromwell also disapproved—in public, that is. Behind the scenes the leader of the Roundheads maintained a fine crop of broodmares and raced them frequently, though naturally in private company, and, of course, never on a bet.

The man who truly established racing in England was Charles II, the Restoration king, known to his cronies as the "Merry Monarch." Charles loved everything fast, stimulating, and profitable, and hence he loved the horses. One of his first acts as monarch was to erect a palace on the site of the now-razed King's House and to bring a celebrated riding master, Foubert, from France to train his stallions. Charles made himself an expert on horses and was famous for his uncanny ability to discern a horse's strengths and weaknesses with a single glance. At times he would treat his always lavish entourage to a display of royal sportsmanship by entering the races himself.

In the next century Queen Anne bred horses, commissioned the first General Stud Book, and initiated the giving of cash prizes for winners. Still, horse racing was far from being a universally popular sport. Though sponsored by royalty, the races were for the average track-goer a jostling and at times raucous affair. Grandstands were in use, as were many other track facilities we know today. But the actual running area was ill-defined, with crowds often discarding mounds of refuse onto the so-called course, forcing track officials to erect detours for the horses. Mounted spectators had the habit of following the contestants as they ran, and it was not infrequent for the rider entered in a race to grow bored with the whole thing, turn his horse around, and head for home. Indeed, the race itself was sometimes just one of several featured amusements of the day. At every track conjurers worked cups and balls, prostitutes peddled their fineries, young bloods picnicked, gambled, drank, and wenched. Bear-baiting contests growled on loudly behind the stands, as did bullbaitings. Records tell of a race held at one English course in which three jesters dressed in yellow and blue pajamas huffed and rocked their way a furlong's distance mounted on nothing more than wooden hobby horses. So madcap did the scene at times become that a town magistrate was once forced to post the following bill: "Anyone caught trying to steal or otherwise molest the horses or

their riders in this race shall be punished according to full extent of law."

The unbecoming reputation of horse racing was remediable. One of those responsible for dignifying it was William, Duke of Cumberland, known to eighteenth-century English loyalists as Sweet William and to Scots who suffered his barbarities at Culloden as Stinking Billy. ("Your Highness," a lieutenant replied when ordered by Cumberland to shoot down a helpless prisoner, "I am a soldier, not an executioner.") Off the war ground this nobleman was somewhat more sporting, at least when it came to horses. These he passionately admired, and in 1764 he began to breed them, that same year producing a horse with a temperament as mean as his own, a horse named Eclipse.

For three years the Duke attempted to break Eclipse, always without success. Finally he gave up trying and sold the horse at auction to a man named O'Kelly, who then took two more years to get Eclipse to the point where he would accept a saddle. By this time the horse was already five years old and had never raced. But experience and age mattered nothing to Eclipse. In his first outing as a runner he won by such an enormous number of lengths that onlookers began to laugh, believing the whole thing had been staged by a clumsy fixer. In the next race the same thing occurred, however, and in the next, and in the next. Eclipse, clearly, was no ordinary animal.

Eclipse went on to win twenty-six straight races and eleven King's Plates. Such statistics do him inadequate justice though. His number of wins would have been far greater were it not for the fact that after he beat most of England's finest racers by ridiculous distances no owner dared send his horses against him. Whenever Eclipse ran, the odds were invariably better than 1 to 100

"At the Fair Grounds," 1890 lithograph by Currier & Ives, shows that Victorian America also enjoyed its day at the races. Harness race goes full tilt around track (note large wheels on sulkies) while prize livestock and vegetables are displayed in foreground.

in his favor, because few bettors were willing to put their money against him. "Eclipse first, the rest nowhere," was the popular saying. Forced to retire when no one would compete, Eclipse then proceeded to sire a family that ultimately produced more than three hundred and fifty winning horses. When this phenomenal animal died in 1789 at the age of twenty-five an autopsy showed his hind-leg muscles to be of unparalleled size and his heart the largest ever found inside a horse. "He was never beat," a contemporary relates, "never had a whip on him, never felt the tickling of a spur, nor was he for a moment distressed by the speed or rate of a competitor—outfooting, outstriding and outlasting every horse which started against him."

The enthusiasm generated by Eclipse's superlative performance almost single-handedly propelled horse racing into front-row prominence. The Jockey Club had been formed in 1750, and by 1800 it ruled English racing with an iron hand, giving the sport true respectability. It began the General Stud Book in 1791 and still continues to publish it regularly. The Stud Book is recognized worldwide as the official record of the genealogy of thoroughbred horses. It established that all thoroughbreds are descended from three stallions—Matchen, Herod, and Eclipse—and therefore all thoroughbreds in existence now stem from these great horses. The racing urge spread across Britain, then to the colonies. America, for one, soon began to rival the mother country in its enthusiasm for horses.

Horses had been imported to the colonies as early as 1621. A contemporary record tells of "sack cattle, both horses, mares, cowes, bulls and goates as are shipped to Mr. Craddock." Within twenty years after their arrival these horses were being borrowed from the farm and placed in the paddock. Soon the Newmarket course at

COPYRIGHT 1890, BY CURRIER & IVES, N.Y.

115 NASSAU ST NEW YORK

THE FAIR GROUNDS.

Hempstead Plains, Long Island, was erected, the first real race course in America. Today Belmont Park stands not far from this site. As in seventeenth- and eighteenth-century England, American races were casual affairs with few track rules, no supervision or Jockey Club, and for that matter, no jockeys, as the owners always rode their own steeds.

The original purpose of racing in early America was quite different from that of today. At this time betting was only a minor part of racing and, surprisingly enough, so was the entertainment value. Horses were a standard part of American life, as important as the ax or plow, and the breeding of speed and intelligence was of foremost concern. These first horse races were thus basically proving grounds for quality in horses. The runners with the best track efforts commanded the highest stud fees. As a trainer of the time writes, races were run "not so much for the divertisement of youth as for encouraging the bettering of the breed of horses."

Such lofty motivations lasted only a short while, however. By 1800 the track was already mother to the gamblers, the sharks, the touts, tipsters, and hipsters. Bookmaking developed early in that century and was often taken to sophisticated lengths, especially in New York City, where in 1870 an estimated $15 million was bet every year.

By the 1880s enormous race tracks were under construction, and by the turn of the century racing was the most popular spectator sport in America. Nor have things changed since then. With the advent in many states of off-track betting, and with modern breeding advances, the horses are ever more a subject of fascination, still as intriguing to the modern American as they once were to the ancient Egyptians.

153

A Day at the Races

Horse racing is far and away the most popular betting sport in America. The twenty-five million or so enthusiasts who actually go to the track each year are just for starters. Another ten million make off-track bets. A comparable number place their coin with bookies. In 1974 the recorded amount wagered at the track was $4 billion. Several million dollars often are bet at a single track on a single day. And that is just the recorded amount.

Surprisingly, although racing attracts more plungers than practically all other betting sports combined, it is really a pretty bad gamble. On any given day only 33 percent of bettors walk away from the track with more money than they came with. This leaves 67 percent losers, a poor statistic. Why, then, do people continue to crowd through the turnstiles?

The reason is that other gambling events, especially those at the casino, are rigid, mathematically locked in. No one can beat them because no one can beat arithmetic. This every gambler knows, and he approaches the tables with the realization that he is bucking a mechanical, nonhuman, and occasionally inhuman foe.

The track is something different. There are odds here too, yes, but they are calculated on the quite fallible *opinion* of other bettors. This is because, as we shall see, the parimutuel system is basically a money pool in which the odds are established by the way in which the bettors bet, not by some inexorable law of mathematical probability, as in the casino. Further, a thousand seemingly friendly aids exist along the way to help the horseplayer come into the money. There are racing guides, tout sheets, newspaper handicappers, hot tipsters. The bettor is informed of each horse's life history through past performance and vital statistics charts in *Racing Form* newspapers. Nothing is withheld. There are no secrets. Even the track is seemingly on his side. It takes its percent no matter which horses win, so it obligingly keeps the bettor well informed and the races carefully supervised.

All of these factors make the horseplayer feel that he is dealing with something less than automatic; and despite the fact that statistics show he will lose just as big, or bigger, than in the casino, he trusts in the fact that with the horses he has escaped the inexorability of the odds, that by study and experimentation he will scientifically dope out winners. Perhaps so, at least on a personal basis. There are those who have beat the races. Horseplayers do die broke. But the individual horseplayers, well, some of them have died rich, too. How they did it is anyone's guess. Those who know don't speak, and those who speak don't know. Like all horseplayers, winners or losers, they followed the basic guidelines of the game. The following section provides these guidelines.

Handicapping

This is the technique of collecting information pertinent to a coming race and using it to predict the race's outcome. Here we have the guts of the horse game. Without this skill a bettor might as well choose his horse by throwing darts at a list of entries. This is because racing is the most complicated of betting sports, involving not only the two most unpredictable phenomena we know—man and animal—but also a maddeningly long list of psychological, physiological, and environmental factors that include, to name a few, the records of a horse's past performance, its physical condition and position in the race, its sex, age, and class, its jockey, its trainer, the track condition, the weather, and more. To be a good horse-picker one must make order out of this stew of facts and then, based on an overall vision, come to intelligent conclusions. A handicapper is, therefore, a puzzle-solver,

some would say of the most brilliant kind.

When one sits down to handicap, he sifts and winnows. Which facts are important to the race, he asks himself, and which are not. The information he finally decides to use depends on his method. For some, everything is a tip-off, from the horse's remote ancestry to the names of the jockeys who have been aboard in its last ten outings. For others, and this includes a majority of handicappers and systems players, there are particular keys to picking a winner. Briefly, they are:

Speed. Speed is, after all, what it is all about. One of the first things a handicapper must do is study the speed statistics of each horse and determine, with some calculations of his own, how fast each thoroughbred really is. Speed can be deceptive, though. Certain horses have early speed but languish in the stretch. Some start poorly then finish strong, while still others are swift as the wind in mud but die on a healthy track. Also, since the horse is a living, changing creature his speed varies, too. So most handicappers look for speed statistics that have been compiled no more than a month prior to the race.

Speed Ratings

A special system has been devised by horsemen for evaluating a horse's true track speed. This system is called the "speed rating." To find it the handicapper first assigns a value of 100 to whatever the track record may be in a particular distance. Then he subtracts one point from this 100 value for every 1/5 of a second that a horse has finished short of that record. Thus, if a track record for a six-furlong race is 1:09 and a winner is clocked at 1:10, that horse's speed rating will be 95. Speed ratings are assigned to a horse for every race and are one of the most important of the handicapper's tools.

Text continued on page 164

Familiar sequence at any track on any race day: Selecting winners, giving jockey a leg up in paddock before race, railbirds expressing elation or anguish. Opposite: No. 4 horse lunges into lead at clean start of 10-horse race.

*People watching horses: The thundering
herd (below r) is running at historic Saratoga
in upstate New York, the fans are winning
and losing everywhere. Ground view of race gives
an idea of the speed, power, and danger involved
in riding one half-ton horse among many.*

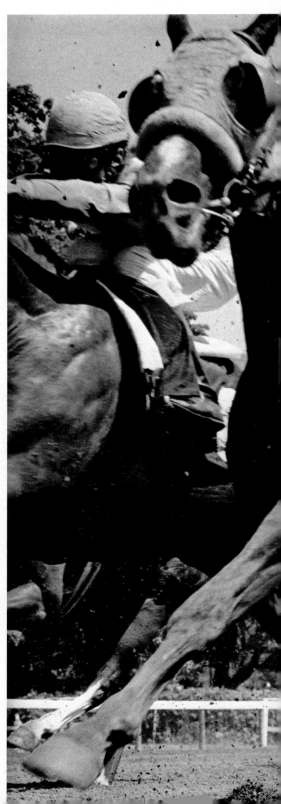

Number 6 leads closely
bunched pack by half a length
and delights fans at Aqueduct
Raceway in New York, where
season's outstanding horses
are often determined.

Weight. The actual weight a horse must carry throughout a race is another key factor, especially significant in a handicap race where superior runners are obliged to carry more weight than their less gifted competitors. The assigned weight is reached by slipping lead weights into pockets under the saddle flaps. This addition is designed to equalize the runners' chances; but in truth what it does is give the handicapper another headache, forcing him to dope out the relationship that exists between a horse's native speed and its carrying capacity. Although a few betting handicappers prefer to put their heads in the sand, ignoring the weight factor completely, most agree that even a slight increase can at times break a horse. Generally the rule is that the longer the race and the greater the addition to the horse's accustomed load, the more the weight factor will work against him.

Class. Class means just that: value, ability, the overall quality of a horse as determined both by his breeding and by his past record as a racer, and expressed in terms of its monetary worth. A horse may be in the $2,000 class, the $3,500 class, and so forth. Now, although the horse's world is a class-structured society, there is still plenty of mobility within the matrix. In most cases horses are classified by their owners or trainers through the medium of claiming races. For example, in a $5,000 claiming race, any horse may be claimed for $5,000. If the owner thought the horse was worth more, he would enter him in a higher-priced race. Owners are constantly raising and dropping their steeds to different classes as a means of determining which niche these horses belong in, and the smart handicapper is on the lookout for such shifts. When a loser is dropped in class his poor record must be

reevaluated in the light of his new and less distinguished competition; and when a horse with a dazzling record is raised in class he must be reviewed with the knowledge that his competition will be sharper as well.

Past Record. All the statistics of a horse's past perform-ance are vital information to the horseman. He consults the newspaper, the *Racing Form,* the tout sheets. He studies a horse's won-and-lost record, its position at differ-ent stages of a race, its running time and speed ratings, its health, past earnings, the record of its workouts, the horses it has beaten or lost to, the distances it has run, its age, sex, stable, post position, skills on different tracks.

After he has taken all these factors into account, he translates the information into prophecy. Which of these factors he will give the most credit to and which he will skim depends on his handicapping technique and whether or not he favors a system. Whatever his method, however, the records of past performance remain the most important set of statistics for evaluating a horse.

The Jockey. A controversial question in handicapping: Does the jockey affect the horse's chances of winning, and if so, how much? Disagreement is rife. The truth is, though, that good jockeys win more consistently than poor jockeys. In fact, in 1974 2 percent of all jockeys won 20 percent of all races, a significant figure. Perhaps it can be said that a jockey is good because he rides good horses. But then how does a jockey earn this privilege without riding a lot of winners before his reputation is established? It is a complicated question, too. Some jockeys are best in a sprint, others over long distances. Some ride well in rain, others are best on a dry track. Generally a good jockey rides a good race. That's the best rule to follow.

The Parimutuel

The dictionary defines the parimutuel as "a system of betting on races whereby the winners divide the total amount bet, after deducting management expenses." Unfortunately the dictionary has neglected to mention a couple of things. First, that the *state*, as well as the management, takes "deductions." And second, that management pockets a little extra above and beyond its regular deductions. All winnings are rounded off to the nearest the whole number and the "odd change" in between reverts to the track. This is "breakage."

Yet despite the fact that the parimutuel exists only to earn profit for the parimutuel and that horseplayers die broke, etc., the parimutuel is still a rather remarkable not-unfair affair. It was dreamed up by a Parisian perfume manufacturer, Pierre Oller. In 1865 Oller was asked by a bookmaker friend to invent a system whereby the bookmaker would profit no matter *how* the bettor bet and no matter *how* the horses ran. Oller considered the matter,

then remembered the age-old concept of the betting pool in which all the money placed by all the bettors was divided proportionately among all the winners. Using this idea as a springboard, Oller suggested that the amount of payoff money on a winning race ticket be determined by the sum of money bet on the winning horse in relation to the money bet on all other horses in the race—and that while this money was being divided among the winners, the bookmaker should take a certain percentage for his trouble. *Voila!* The parimutuel.

It was an idea whose time had come, and before long machines capable of tallying the mathematics of such transactions were in existence. Though something of a success in Europe, the system did not come to America until after World War I. The "totalizator" did not catch on until around 1930; it was then put into common use.

The Totalizator

This is more than a machine. It is an event, a living

system, a giant mechanical mind that oversees and controls all aspects of parimutuel betting, doing everything including selling tickets. Basically, its jobs are to take care of the printing, issuing, and redeeming of all racing tickets; to relay the sales information on ticket buying to a central computer; to compute the unfathomably complex and ever-changing relationships between the bets and the odds; and to transmit all this information electronically to the tote board in the infield, where it is displayed for the coming race. The totalizator, quite clearly, makes the modern parimutuel run.

Touts

Every track has its touts, those Damon Runyonesque fellows with turned-up collars and racing forms tucked under their arms, who are quick to give a hot tip and quick to ask for a tip of a different kind in return. There are a number of men who make livings out of this game, and some of them have not done so badly at it, either.

Despite the official-looking sheets he peddles and despite his sincere assurances of "inside information," however, the tout is rarely privy to private knowledge; if he were would he be eager to share it? Some touts will tip a number of all of the horses in the same race to different bettors. One of them will win and pay off the tout one way or another. On the other hand, some touts are excellent handicappers, many of them literally having grown up at the track. Their success, which occasionally is considerable, is due to this long apprenticeship with the horses. So if you must follow a tout and his tout sheet, follow one who has a good record.

Systems

It has been estimated, probably without exaggeration, that there are more than a thousand systems today for

selecting and betting race horses. The nature of the beast makes it so, for there are innumerable variables in this game and practically every one has at different times served as the foundation for a system. One man bases his method on weight, another on the jockey, a third on stretch gains, a fourth on earnings, a fifth on underlay-overlay, a sixth on consistency . . . and so on.

Systems arose no doubt from the track-goer's discontent with professional handicappers and from a disillusionment with handicapping in general. Handicapping and system play, it is important to note, differ in real ways. The handicapper analyzes the full spectrum of a horse's past performance. The system player finds only one or several factors important enough to determine a winner; and if he does not ignore all other factors in his reckonings then he keeps them thoroughly subordinate.

Systems are often misunderstood. No track-goer in his right mind believes, as might a blackjack enthusiast or crap shooter, that he is someday going to find a method that will win for him each time out or, for that matter, give him anything close to an even chance. This is nonsense. The sensible horseplayer knows that the odds will always be against him and that a good system simply increases his chances of winning by a few percentage points. It is this small addition, however, that makes a system worthwhile. It definitely *is* possible to increase winnings at the track. It *is* possible to make money by playing a system. The requirements are study, experimentation, willingness to take a chance.

The systems presented here are, with a few exceptions, relatively common, having been used by professionals for many years. Each one is relatively simple. There are other types of systems which take up chapters in racing books and even whole books. Many horseplayers believe that the simpler the system the better.

"Steeplechase" derives from straight-line, cross-country race toward distant spire by 19th-century fox hunters. Fence-ditch-hedge obstacles—and inevitable spills—are preserved in modern steeplechases at Kempton Park, England (top), and Saratoga (bottom).

Things To Know About The Races

1. Types of races

Claiming race. *In a claiming race each horse is entered at a "claiming price," which means that at the completion of the race anyone may "claim," or buy, him at the established price. To do this, the buyer, must have deposited the claiming price in advance at the racing secretary's office.*

Optional claiming race. *This is like the claiming race, except that not all the horses are for sale.*

Handicap race. *The owner enters his horse in a handicap race by paying an entry fee. Once enrolled, each horse is assigned certain weights by the track handicapper (this weight is provided by lead weights inserted into the saddle cloth) in order to equalize differences in ability. Thus, a horse judged superior will carry more weight than one less well endowed.*

Allowance race. *This is similar to the handicap race, except that the amount of weight is assigned by rules taken from the condition book rather than by the track handicappers.*

Match race. *A race usually held between two top horses, with the owners putting up large front money, and usually winner-take-all.*

Stake race. *Usually for two- or three-year-olds only. All horses carry the same amount of weight. The entrance fee is much higher than for an allowance or claiming race, and the horses entered are ordinarily top runners.*

Maiden race. *All the entries are "maidens," that is, horses that have never won a race.*

2. Types of bets

Win ticket. *Bettor collects if his horse comes in first.*

Place ticket. *Bettor collects if his horse comes in first or second with, of course, an appropriate decrease in payoff from the win ticket.*

Show ticket. *Bettor collects if his horse comes in first, second, or third, with a decrease in winnings from both win and place tickets.*

Combination tickets. *Win, place, and show, all bet together on one ticket.*

Daily double. *A bet placed in the first and second race of the day, or in the fifth and sixth. The winnings from the first are bet on the second, with the winners collecting payoffs much larger than on an ordinary single bet.*

Quiniela. *The bettor collects if the two horses he has bet on come in first and second, in either order, in the same race. As in the daily double, the payoff is greater than on a single horse bet. The quiniela is but one of a number of new types of bets, all of which involve multiple choice. The rage for these bets started when certain double- and triple-action bets payed off in hundreds of thousands of dollars. (On April 21, 1972, a multiple combination paid $111,912 at Yonkers Raceway.) The result was the institution of a number of multiple ("exotic") bets, including the superfecta (naming the first four horses in their exact order of finish), the trifecta (naming the first three horses in order of finish), and the exacta (first two horses in order of finish).*

3. Types of Horses

Mare. *A female horse of five years or more.*

Colt. *A male horse of four years or younger.*

Gelding. *A male horse of any age that has been castrated.*

Ridgling. *A male horse that has been partially castrated.*

Filly. *A female horse four years or younger.*

Dam. *A mare that has given birth.*

Yearling. *A horse that is one year old.*

Foal. *A new-born horse.*

Entire horse. *A male horse five years or older that has not been gelded.*

Juvenile. *A horse that is two years old.*

Sire. *The male parent of a horse.*

Stallion. *An adult male horse that has not been castrated.*

Smart-money Playdown. If a newspaper handicapper rates a horse at, say, 9 to 1 odds, and if these odds open lower the day of the race and continue to drop suddenly and inexplicably right before post time, bet on this horse and bet on him to win. Chances are that a lot of smart money with inside information has been holding back till the last minute. The odds say that an underlay will win one time out of four, not too bad an average.

Past Winners. This is really a simple one: Bet on the horse that won the last time out, especially if it won coming on strong in the stretch. This means it probably is reaching the top of its form. If more than one repeater is entered in a race, study each one's performance records. If they all seem worthwhile then bet each across the board. Or if you want to make a single bet, choose the winning horse that had the better speed record over the same distance.

Old Reliable. This is another easy one that takes little practice to put into operation. It is based on scanning the info sheets for the *reliable* horse, the *consistent* horse, and then putting your money on it. But be careful. Make certain that the chosen horse has not been raised in class for this race; and be sure that it is thoroughly familiar with the distance it will run that day.

Betting the Favorite. This may seem like an obvious method and it probably is. But so what? The point of a system is to help the bettor win, and not to be original. All that is necessary in this approach is to keep abreast of the information available on the horses and to follow the suggestions of the most accurate handicappers. Most newspaper handicappers are informed bettors. They know their stuff. If several of them agree on the merits of a certain horse then use their experience to your advantage. The only time to pull back is when the favorite has some unusual handicap working, such as running an unfamiliar distance, a mare running against males, an injury. Otherwise betting the favorite is probably the safest system for betting winners. Bettors who follow this system are known as "chalk players."

Good Luck in Threes. This is a system strictly for the mystically inclined, and it comes without a promise. It is based on an ancient and uncannily persistent notion that all things good and bad come in triplicate, wins at the race track included. If a horse has won the last two times out, bet on him to win again. You might be surprised.

Betting the Jockey. If a good jockey is riding a good horse this improves that good horse's chances of winning. Statistics say so. Certain jockeys win as many as 30 percent of their races, an abnormally high number. Find out who they are, follow them, and bet them to win. If a generally losing jockey is riding a winning horse, forget it, at least as far as this system goes. And if a good jockey is riding a loser, don't commit yourself till you have all the details. Study all the information you can get concerning this horse, especially the record of its recent workouts and its stretch gains. There may be gold hidden in the dross, for when a horse of no particular distinction is suddenly assigned a prominent jockey this may mean that its owner feels it is "ready."

Class. There are two ways to bet the class system, the rise in class and the drop in class. Those who bet on a dropped horse believe that since its owner has dropped it from, say, a $4,000 class to a $2,000 class he must have high hopes for it making money in a lower position. If this horse has been riding against decent competition and doing not too badly, this is an especially important indication. It means that the dropped horse may well clean up against lesser competitors. Some system players simply bet the horse that has had the largest drop. Others bet dropped horses only if they once raced good competition.

The other type of class-system player is the raised-class bettor. Whenever the *Racing Form* tells of a horse raised in class, many horseplayers will zero in, taking this to mean that the owner has plans for his animal, that he feels the time has come for a big win. One thing, though. Any good system player will never bet blindly one way all the time, rise or drop. A rise in class may be good in some instances, bad in others. Bear in mind that for thirty days after a horse is claimed, his class is raised by at least 25 percent. That is not in his favor. It all depends on the read-out from *all* the information. People who mechanically bet the same way without taking the variables into consideration usually bet losers.

Harness Racing

Since its humble beginnings at midwestern county fairs, harness racing has become one of the fastest growing spectator sports in the United States. In a standardbred race, the horse pulls a sulky and driver, and must pace or trot—but not run, canter, or gallop. Most horse bettors find it easier to pick the winner of a harness race than a thoroughbred race. We'll discuss the principle factors of harness-race handicapping.

Class. This is a very fluid quality in the life of the average standardbred racehorse. When the animal is at the peak of its shape cycle (in top physical condition), it will be racing at a class level several notches higher than normal; when at the bottom of its shape cycle, it will be racing several notches lower. Class is not an absolute "thing" that a horse either has or doesn't have. Horses that, as youngsters, competed in the top echelon, may slip to the very lowest claiming ranks later in life.

Speed. Harness horses do not go all out for the duration of the distance; they go rated miles. For this reason, mile clockings are deceptive. There exists among standardbreds—unlike thoroughbreds—the phenomenon of the so-called "suck-along" clocking in which a horse of modest ability is "carried," as it were, by better horses to a faster mile time than he could ever have accomplished on his own!

Driver Strategy. The driver of a harness horse is much more important to the outcome than the jockey aboard a thoroughbred racehorse. This is especially true when the scene of action is a half-mile oval characterized by four sharp turns to the mile. Here, driver strategy is at a premium, and the game becomes one of various "moves," as follows:

1. A sharp early move to front, in order to establish a favorable striking position, known as "leaving the gate."

2. A "quarter" move, executed after a quarter of a mile, in which the object is to gain the lead with a minimum of strain on the horse in a usually slow second quarter.

3. The driver can attempt to "loop the field" with a "three-wide sweep" in the backstretch, hoping to take his opponents by complete surprise.

4. The driver can also "hang 'em out to dry" by refusing to give up the lead and dueling his rivals into the ground—often ruining his own chances as well—with a fast quarter.

These are just some of the ways a driver can try to win the race. The strategies are varied and complex, underscoring the truism that in harness racing, the teamster is truly in the driver's seat. Indeed, some fans say that it is more of a driver's game than a horse's game. But the fact remains that even a great driver will finish unplaced if he has "no horse."

Weight. In thoroughbred racing, weight is the great equalizer. In harness racing, it is for the most part irrelevant. With thoroughbreds, the weight of a jockey is on the horse's back. With standardbreds, the weight is be-

hind the horse; he merely pulls it along on bicycle tires —and not from a standing start as a thoroughbred must do, but at a full gait of 25 mph just before the race begins.

It is nevertheless true that a 125-pound driver will usually have something of an edge over a 225-pound driver, all other things being equal. Most of the best drivers in the country have been in the 150-pound range, although there have been a few highly successful reinsmen who tipped the beam at 200 pounds.

Distance. Thoroughbreds run anywhere from two furlongs to two miles, with races between five furlongs and one and one-eighth miles most commonly seen. These distances can be negotiated on either dirt or turf. With only rare exceptions, standardbreds race one mile on the dirt. Indeed, the very name "standardbred" refers to the time-standards that were earlier established for the mile distance.

Post Position. In thoroughbred racing, this factor is a minor one. In harness racing, it exerts a major influence on the outcome of races, and doubly so on half-mile tracks. Many systems have been devised on post position alone, although none of them are recommended to readers of this book.

Why is post position so important on half-mile harness tracks? First, it is important because the shortest distance from start to finish is along the inner rail, and the horse in post position number one has the advantage of already being there when the race starts. (In harness racing, as in auto racing, this coveted spot is known as the "pole position.")

Second, it is important because post position creates a natural order of early running position. This determines which horses will be near the front or far in the back—unless, of course, a driver has used a strategy to counteract a bad post position, but even that could take its toll.

Text continued on page 185

Harness racing is significantly affected by driver, post position, and sulky. Driver can be more important than jock because of many turns in short tracks. Post position (opposite) favors rail horse, works against No. 8 "out there." Lighter sulky, modified in 1976, has cut seconds off times.

At Epsom Downs (1), as elsewhere
in England, horses run clockwise
on grassy track. British also
favor steeplechases—obstacle
races for gentleman jockeys—
more than the rest of the world.
Above: Bookmaking is legal
and colorful oddsmakers are
much in evidence at meets.

Most famous race in U.S. is Kentucky Derby at Churchill Downs for 3-year-olds. Left: Crowd jams infield. Right: Bettors ignore CBS. Below l: At 20 minutes to post time No. 2 is a 5-1 choice. Below: No. 2—Secretariat, Ron Turcotte up—rewards chalk players in driving finish.

In a standard eight-horse field, the outermost position number eight is the worst. On average, horses win only one-fourth as often from "out there" as they do from the pole position. Therefore, it would seem that the odds against a horse winning from post number eight would be four times higher than from the number one position. In general, that is true, but if the horse is a "frontrunner" (as opposed to a "closer"), his chances might not be that bad if he can establish a contending position from the outset without expending too much energy.

Consistency. Standardbreds are much more durable than thoroughbreds; therefore they are more consistent. The average harness horse races 30 times a year, and it is common to see 40 or 45 annual starts for a standardbred racer over a period of many years. In a sense, these animals are like machines. When they race, their time is often within a few fifths of a second of their best mile time for half-a-dozen races in a row. A thoroughbred that races 40 or 45 times in a single season soon becomes known as an "iron horse."

Once a standardbred achieves his best form, he will hold it for a long period of time. If seen on a graph, the cycle from dull to sharp to dull form would be a gradual arc. A thoroughbred's cycle is of much shorter duration, and might even consist of radical zigzags from one race to another.

Equipment. Harness racing was revolutionized in 1976 with the arrival of Joe King's modified sulky. Designed by an aerodynamics engineer, the new "bike," as it is known, has improved horses' mile clockings by as much as two full seconds. The reasons for this are still being debated, but there is general agreement that the new sulky is more comfortable for a horse than the old, heavier conventional sulky. It takes the weight of the driver's legs and sulky shafts off the horse's front feet and actually puts it under the horse's chest. The animal is lighter up front, and tires less readily. The modified sulky also cuts down on wind resistance and helps horses to negotiate the turns better. Now used by 95 percent of all standardbreds at major harness tracks, it looks as though King's invention is here to stay.

Track Size. Harness tracks come in three sizes: 1-mile oval, ⅝-mile oval, ½-mile oval. By far the most popular size is the ½-mile oval, simply because the fans see the horses three times during the running of the race—at the start, at the half-mile pole, at the finish line. Some purists maintain that 1-mile tracks provide a truer test for the horses, but it is not very exciting as the horses are far removed from the spectators for much of the running. A reasonable attempt to combine the best features of the ½-mile and 1-mile ovals are the ⅝-mile tracks with three turns to the mile.

Age and Sex. The Jockey Club Scale of Weights serves to equalize age and sex differences among thoroughbreds. A 3-year-old filly, for example, would get a 22-pound weight advantage if she were competing with older males in the month of April at a distance of one mile. As the year progresses, her weight advantage would be decreased by a few pounds each month. The assumption is that she is getting bigger and stronger as the months go by, and therefore able to compete on a gradually more equal footing with older males.

Among standardbred racehorses, there is no such provision for females. A 3-year-old filly can and does defeat older males without the benefit of any special allowances, if she has the speed and class to do so. Indeed, 2-year-olds—mere babies—have been known to whip the hobbles off seasoned veterans. In thoroughbred circles, this would be unheard of in our era (although not in the previous century, curiously enough).

Trotters at Yonkers Raceway, New York (left), complete first of two laps. No. 4 horse (lying 6th) eventually won, paying $3.80. Note difference in stride of these trotters compared with pacers below, which move pair of legs on either side in unison.

On the pacing gait, age and sex are clearly not relevant factors. On the *trotting* gait, however, it is a fact that females actually have an advantage over their male rivals, everything else being equal. Of the top three money-winning trotters of all time, *all* are females!

This is no accident. Observers of the sport say that it is the wider pelvis of the female that gives her greater leverage than the male when competing on the trot. She covers more ground and has a greater reach, all with less effort. On the pacing gait, her wide pelvis affords no advantage, and from the mechanistic viewpoint she competes on equal footing with males.

A Betting Viewpoint

For intelligent horseplayers, the "law" for guidance in making a correct betting decision is this: there is an inverse ratio between performance and payoff strength. In other words, generally speaking, the more a horse "stands out" in his field, the shorter his price will be. Therefore, a positive advantage on the *handicapping* side becomes neutralized on the *betting* side when the horse's merits are obvious to the majority of players. The weight of their own money has created an "underlay" situation.

The astute bettor will be ever conscious of such trends in the tote, and he will refuse to speculate on propositions that offer a potential return on investment that does not justify the risk. He is looking for favorable investments, and he knows that only "overlays" can qualify as such. Horses held in the tote market at odds which are *less* than their apparent chances of victory (i.e. "underlays") will be avoided at all costs. Those held at odds which are *more* than their apparent chances warrant (i.e. "overlays") are the ones to wait for.

A horse that is neither underlaid nor overlaid, but held at apparently correct odds—a so-called

Opposite: English bookie pays off
successful bettor. These happy transactions
occur after every race, but only for
favored few. Below: Experienced eye of horse
player scans Racing Form far
from sights and sounds of track.

"equalay," for its apparent chances are *equal* to the odds offered—could hardly qualify as an attractive wagering proposition. This is because the long-term margin of profit, excluding progression, will be nonexistent in such betting transactions.

Overlays alone suffice to "guarantee," as it were, a long-term rate of profit on investment. This "guarantee" is contingent upon the individual player's handicapping abilities, however. If, as a perceptive analyst, he can estimate win-chances among a field of racehorses better than the aggregated, leveled-down collectivity of the parimutuel betting public, then there is no reason why a player can't derive profits from race speculation by exploiting parimutuel "imbalances" to his or her personal betting advantage.

It goes without saying that patience is required to wait for overlay opportunities in a horse race. The average nine- or ten-race card will yield no more than two or three legitimate overlays; thus the majority of races, roughly 7 out of 10 on average, will be passed in favor of a more lucrative betting opportunity late on the card.

The general racegoing public has little ability to discriminate between a good wager and a poor one. In the majority of races, they settle upon a horse whose odds *do not* compare favorably with his chances—paradoxically through the influence on their own money in the parimutuel marketplace. By doing so, they get shortchanged at the cashier's window when they do manage to pick a winner.

Many players think that handicapping involves picking winners, but that is true only indirectly. The proper task of handicapping is not to pick winners—it is to *assign chances*, or estimate the win probability for *each* horse in a race—and *then* pick the horse to wager upon . . . *after* the odds for each contestant are known.

This is done by comparing one's *own* priceline with toteboard prices as near to post-time as possible and "buying" the best-value horse(s) in the race on the basis of what could be called "comparison shopping." The successful horsegambler is looking for overlays— horses whose odds are higher than their estimated chances of winning.

If nothing in the race is overlaid, the "pro" passes the event in favor of a later race on the card. He is not hungry for action; he possesses the discipline to wait for the most favorable betting opportunities, even if it means sitting out four or five races in a row.

Amateurs operate differently. First, they seldom if ever pass a race, and then only if they are broke, confused beyond reason as to the outcome, or get shut out. They want action in every race, including all kinds of gimmick wagering. Second, they try to pick the likeliest winner of the race—the horse with the best single chance—paying only secondary attention to the risk-reward potentiality of the transaction.

Each of these mistakes is serious enough to prevent bettors from showing a worthwhile profit in their long-term wagering activities. True, they might get very lucky on any given day or night, or even for an entire season, but in the end players who play the game in the wrong way will pay the piper. Unless, of course, they learn how to handicap and bet correctly, which involves developing a long-term outlook along with the patience to wait for overlays.

Man Versus Machine

When you bet legally at a racetrack, you bet with a machine. When you bet illegally away from the track, you bet with a man. That man is known as a "bookie," and if he knows you as a regular customer, there is little that he won't do for you, including lend you money to keep you in action. No machine ever did that.

Bookmakers extend credit to their clientele. The parimutuel machine demands cash in the barrelhead.

Bookmakers offer bets on a number of different tracks in your area of the country. The parimutuel machine limits you to the racing program at your local track.

Bookmakers provide "gimmick" wagers of every description, such as "parlays," "round-robins," "if bets," "back to back," "in reverse"—some of which, when successfully completed, seem to require the assistance of a accountant to tabulate the winnings.

Bookmakers give their customers a bottle of whiskey or a box of fine cigars at Christmas time.

Bookmaking is illegal.

Inscrutable, undaunted, his mental
computer whirring as sixth race threatens,
the genus Horse player—*subspecies*
Newyork—*plays out the string*
on a snowy afternoon at the track.

A Short Dictionary of Horse Racing

Across the board. *Betting win, place, and show on the same horse in the same race.*

Break. *When a pacer or trotter goes off stride and begins to gallop or buck-jump, the horse is said to be "in a break."*

Breakage. *The amount of money left over after the track pays off winnings, determined by figuring payoff sums to a round figure. For instance, if the payoff is $5.63 the winner gets $5.60 and the track gets three cents—"breakage."*

Brush. *When a standardbred makes its move.*

Calls. *The position of a horse during the various stages of the race.*

Closer. *A horse that comes on strong at the finish of a race, that "closes" in on his competition.*

Colors. *Silk shirt and cap worn by a jockey, the color and pattern of which signify a particular owner and stable.*

Condition book. *Schedule of races kept by the track secretary.*

Cover. *Protection from the wind when racing behind another horse.*

First over. *The first horse to challenge the pacesetter from the outside, or on the "overland," is said to be "first over(land)." Generally this is the toughest move for a horse to succeed in making.*

Furlong. *Two hundred twenty yards or one-eighth of a mile.*

Furlong pole. *Marker situated one-eighth of a mile before the finish line.*

Handicap. *The amount of weight a horse is assigned to carry in a handicap race.*

Hand ride. *A ride in which a jockey does not use his whip.*

Hot walker. *The man who walks a horse after the race to cool it out and restore its proper body temperature.*

In the money. *A horse that finishes either first, second, or third.*

Jockeys up. *The track official's announcement indicating that it is time for the jockeys to mount their horses.*

Lines. *The reins that a harness racing driver uses to control his horse.*

Lugging. *The tendency of a horse to pull to one side while running.*

Morning glory. *A horse that works out well but does poorly in a race.*

Morning line. *Odds established by racing officials the morning of a particular race.*

Odds-on. *A horse that runs at less than even money.*

Pacer. *A harness horse that is laterally gaited, moving its right-front and right-rear legs simultaneously. (See "Trotter.")*

Paddock. *Area where the horses are saddled before the race.*

Parked out. *A horse that races "two wide" of the inner rail, losing valuable ground on all turns.*

Pocket. *A position occupied by the horse that sits second on the rail behind the pacesetter, the ideal place to be in a harness race.*

Post parade. *Revue of horses and jockeys in front of the grandstand before a race.*

Pulling up. *Maneuver by a jockey to retard a horse after a race.*

Repeater. *A horse that was a winner the last time out, and wins again today.*

Router. *A horse that runs well at a mile or more.*

Scratch. *To withdraw a horse from a race.*

Set-down. *Suspension of a jockey from racing for an infraction of racing rules or ethics, the number of days depending on seriousness of the offense.*

Steward. *Overseer of the race track empowered to arbitrate all disputes and to fine delinquent parties.*

Sulky. *A racing cart upon which the driver sits, also known as a "bike," a "buggy," or a "basket."*

Syndication. *Group ownership of a horse, usually in the form of shares for breeding purposes.*

Three deep. *A horse that is third abreast of the inner railing, or two horse-widths away from the rail. He loses valuable ground, especially when forced to negotiate turns in the third lane.*

Trotter. *A harness horse that is diagonally gaited, moving its right-front and left-rear legs simultaneously, a movement known as "crossfiring." (see "Pacer.")*

Wire. *The finish line.*

Horse Homilies

"The first, and perhaps best, handicapping system ever invented was to take the horse with the best race at the latest date."
Les Conklin, well-known handicapper and racing authority

"Your most difficult problem [in handicapping] will be the psychological roadblock you encounter if you allow yourself to be influenced by the fact that your horse may be at long odds on the 'tote' board. Don't start saying to yourself that all those thousands of spectators who are betting on shorter-priced horses can't be crazy."
Les Conklin

"You can beat a race but you can't beat the races."
Old racing maxim

"People who approach the track as if it were a bingo parlor miss more than a half of the fun. Our motto, if we must have one, is that it is more fun to win than to lose, and even while losing, it is more fun to know what you are doing, rather than sit around watching for the next bulletin from fate."
Tom Ainslie, well-known racing authority

"Before leaving home, decide how much you want to spend [bet], add the track admission price, the price of a program, an allowance for refreshments and the price of your transportation. The total is your budget. Take this amount and no more, so that if you lose you won't be tempted to recoup your losses and lose more than you planned."
John Scarne

"The race is not always to the swift, nor the battle to the strong—but that's the way to bet."
Damon Runyon

"Condition has more to do with a horse winning or losing the race than the weight it carries. A high-class horse couldn't win a race with a feather on his back if he is not in condition."
Pittsburgh Phil, famous horseplayer

"Most of the people who put down their money with him [a bookmaker] don't know what they're doing. Good gambling, whether it's on dice or cards or horses, requires skill. Anybody who bets money on anything in the hope that luck will make him a winner is an idiot. When I was cutting corks I had to know my business to make a living from my job, and the same thing's true of gambling."
Pittsburgh Phil

"If you want to find out which tracks are not run with stress on honesty then there is one simple test. Just get hold of a reliable bookmaker and ask him if he will accept bets on races at Blank Park. If he refuses you can be sure that enough monkey business goes on at this track to make it a fine place to avoid."
Oswald Jacoby

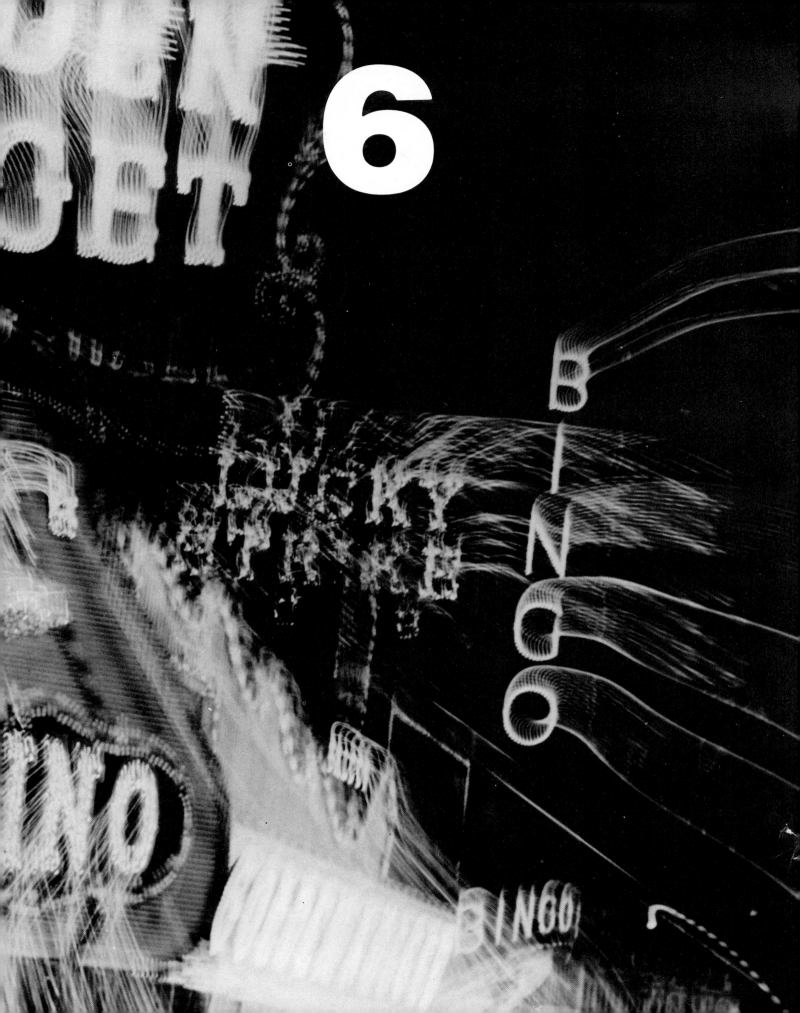

6. Casinos and Arenas

For those who want to wager their money in exotic locations around the world, there are casinos in countries such as Ghana, Lebanon, and Syria. But if you prefer more accessible, better-known places, you can visit gambling establishments in Las Vegas, Monte Carlo, Puerto Rico, the Bahamas, London, and in continental Europe. Of course, the most famous of them all is Monte Carlo. There is no getting away from it. Yet, as has often been pointed out, while Monte Carlo has the tradition, Las Vegas gets the play; and the play, as every gambler agrees, is definitely the thing.

Las Vegas is not all of it. The entire state, all of Nevada, is where the action lies. Within the thin triangle described by those three magic points—Reno, Tahoe, and Vegas—most of the true business is to be found.

Why Nevada?

Granted statehood in 1864, little more than a decade after the start of the California gold rush, Nevada was looked upon as a necessary evil, a place to be suffered while crossing the Sierra Mountains into golden California. During the period of its entrance into the Union, however, the Comstock Lode was discovered, and soon thereafter a number of similarly rich silver deposits appeared. The ugly duckling had become a swan. Now Nevada was just plain necessary, and thousands of travelers stayed on. By 1870 there were eighteen thousand citizens in Virginia City, with one casino for every one hundred fifty inhabitants. Everyone, *everyone*, who had ventured into this arid metal farm had done so for a simple reason: money. Money in mining, money in railroads, money in trading with the Indians, money in silver and gold. From the very beginning Nevada was founded on America's love of the green, and so it was predictable that gambling would become the Nevadan's favorite pastime.

This is why almost every tale told by nineteenth-century travelers passing through Nevada makes some reference to the gaming that took place there. "The quiet and stillness were remarkable," an English journalist noted in 1851 of the inside of a casino. "Nothing was heard but a slight hum of voices and the constant clicking of money."

In 1879 gambling was legalized in Nevada and continued its sanctioned ways up to the turn of the century. Then in 1909 a wave of antigambling sentiment swept across the prairies and the buck stopped in Nevada. The state legislature, forced to bow to the demands of the "progressivists," outlawed the sport. But so ingrained was it among the citizenry that a full-blown gambling underground arose that was impossible to police, and the law had to be modified. In 1931 gambling was once again legalized in Nevada.

While the legalizing processes were underway in this desert state, two other events also were in the works, both of which would augment the glamour. First was the ratification of an easy divorce law, whereby Nevada residents—and this meant anyone who had lived there more than six weeks—could gain an uncomplicated and remarkably speedy divorce. Thousands of divorce-seekers soon flooded Nevada's courts of law, and before long Reno and Las Vegas were the singles capitals of the West.

While the divorce machine was booming, another big draw was under construction not too many miles from Vegas: Hoover Dam, one of the largest building projects ever undertaken. Thousands of workers poured into the area with their families, and cities sprang up overnight in a land that had once been nemesis to the homesteader. The population of Las Vegas doubled in five years.

Then came World War II. Military installations cropped up across the state, and a postwar population

boom followed when the Government moved its nuclear testing facilities forty miles northwest of the city. Las Vegas began to grow for real, and this expansion was in no way impeded by the sudden influx of investments from odd, faraway places like Chicago, Detroit, and Jersey City. The mobs had arrived, and with them came Bugsy Siegel, builder of the first great luxury hotel-casino in the West, the Flamingo. Gunned down as quickly as his project went up, Siegel was the premier victim of gangland in Vegas. A series of other killings followed, and as the gaming palaces accumulated on the Strip, the number of murders increased. In the late 1940s the state government got fed up and moved in. The games were cleaned up, cheating was minimized. A tax was imposed on the casinos' gross revenues and 2 percent of the take went to the state, along with the "table tax" levied on every machine in operation. Casino owners and operators were closely screened before licensing, and a five-man board was established to oversee all gambling activity in the state. By 1950 so much money was pouring into the state's coffers as a result of this clean-up that residents of Nevada no longer paid state income tax.

Surprisingly, the first of Nevada's great casinos was not in Vegas at all but in its northern counterpart, Reno, the "biggest little city in the world." This casino was Harolds Club.

The year was 1937. Gambling was still a product of the Wild West. Casinos were dark, honky-tonk places, their floors covered with sawdust and misses at the spitoon. Fistfights were not uncommon and gunfights were not unknown. The clientele was unsavory and all of it was male—not exactly a spot with much out-of-town draw, and *certainly* no place for the ladies. Raymond Smith, founder and one might say "inventor" of Harolds Club, changed all this. Within the first year of his management he successfully face-lifted his establishment into the twentieth century, modernizing its facilities, lighting up its façade at night, installing plate-glass windows out front so that people could look in and see that *this* casino at least was not the devil's den. Mr. Smith, an ex-carnival barker and a man with a taste for the shocking, then raised more eyebrows by not only allowing women into his gaming emporium, but inviting them . . . and, at the same time, hiring them as dealers, a deed equally impious in this macho community.

This was just the start. Advertising was Mr. Smith's forte. He started by running a roulette game with a mouse as the ball and numbered mouseholes for the wheel. Next came fireworks displays, float parades through the center of town, bonanza releases of helium balloons, tattooed with the club's insignia. More than twenty million club matches were printed. Seven hundred and fifty one-armed bandits were installed, more than one-fifteenth of all the slot machines in Nevada. The dimensions of the casino itself were expanded, with a Wild West museum built to house Smith's collection of western memorabilia, and five saloons constructed nearby, one of them boasting a giant bourbon waterfall that flowed day and night behind the bar.

Of all the stunts ever launched by the industrious Mr. Smith, however, his *pièce de résistance* was the coast-to-coast billboard blitz. Why confine one's reputation to local gentry, the wily promoter asked. Why not implant our moniker in the minds of every living American, the Connecticut Yankee and the Southern Belle, as well as the western dude? After all, four out of five of the five thousand people a day who visit Harolds Club are out-of-staters. Why not take advantage of this fact? By the time World War II had come and gone there was a chain of more than four thousand signs stretching from Miami to Fairbanks, each depicting a covered wagon full of grotesquely drawn pioneers, one of whom calls out to the spectator that for him it is "Harolds Club or Bust." To this day, several teams of construction engineers are kept busy across the country erecting these incredible contributions to Pop culture. And what's more, they work. Since 1946 Harolds Club has been the most successful and the most highly patronized casino in the world.

Las Vegas

If the action in Reno is swift, that in Las Vegas is a torrent. After a trip to this strange and dreamlike city, one is never quite the same. The greatest shock, for many, comes from just seeing Las Vegas for the first time. Having passed most of his day squinting at baked-over prairie and unfriendly, windswept railroad towns, the traveler on the road to Vegas is growing numb. The senses dull. Hours pass. One more range of mountains. Will this trip never end? The descent into a valley. Then . . . all of a sudden . . . from the bosom of absolute nothingness . . . a miracle of spinning lights, a giant coruscating rhinestone in the Sahara—a mirage—Vegas!

By the time the visitor's eyes accustom themselves to this vision, he finds himself several miles south of the city limits, cruising along the famous Strip. Here stand eighteen mammoth hotel-casinos, the largest collection in the world, each with flashing arrows, colossal marquees, revolving neon mannequins, any kind of eye-catching phantasma to lure in the just-arrived traffic trade. Everything along the Strip is sparkly, futuristic, tightly packed. The hotels have discovered that patrons like to gamble in places where many casinos are crowded into one small area, and as a result each hotel stands huddled next to its neighbor with a closeness inappropriate to the great desert spaces around it. This consolidation makes

The Strip: Main stem of Nevada's garish desert flower, Las Vegas, the gambling capital of the world, which offers the most of practically everything and runs full blast day and night. Gambling revenues are so enormous that Nevadans pay no state income taxes.

Las Vegas literally a town without suburbs, a town arising from nowhere at one border and ending just as abruptly at the other.

In Vegas the visito quickly notices that by no means is this a typical American town. First, there are more pawn shops here than in Chicago and New York put together, enough to service all those bettors gone broke. Many of these establishments go by the homey name of "trading posts." But inside the counter receipts look dangerously like pawn tickets. Also in Vegas the newcomer beholds an inordinately large collection of motels. There is one on practically every street corner. It is said that one hundred thousand rooms are always available for business. Now on paper this looks rather odd. There are, after all, only sixty-seven thousand residents in the whole city. When it is discovered, however, that at any given time Vegas has approximately a half million visitors it all makes sense.

There are not only innumerable sleeping accommodations in Vegas, but eating ones abound as well: almost a thousand restaurants of every conventional and exotic persuasion. The cuisine is good here and attractively served, but no longer cheap. At one time the policy among casinos was to charge little for food, drink, and entertainment, the theory being that cheap accommodations would attract more gambling money. It was then learned that patrons came anyway, no matter what things cost. Up went the prices and no one seemed to get hurt.

Some things still are bargains. Weddings, for one. Marriage is as cheap as divorce in Nevada, and can be purchased at any of the emporiums of connubial contract —the marriage parlor—such as the "Honeymooners' Haven," "Ye Olde Marriage Shack," "Marriage, Inc.," and dozens more. In what style do you wish to be wed? Wild West? Elizabethan? New England church? Vine-

covered cottage? There are marriage parlors to suit every taste and pocketbook, ranging from the ten-dollar, ten-minute, over-the-desk special, to the works, complete with flower-decked altar, justice-of-the-peace (no tip required), photographer, and organist. Witnesses will be supplied on request.

Leaving the Strip with its unique allurements and moving on to downtown Las Vegas, the visitor now notices the level of chic appreciably declining. The plushness of the Strip gives way to something slightly lean and desperate. Things are still bright and fast-moving, of course, but there is a certain air of serious business here that one rarely finds in the fancier places. This section is called Glitter Gulch or simply "downtown." The little guy comes to this part of town with his dreams of better luck and of breaking the bank with a dime. In these casinos minimum bets are low, one cent at the slots, ten cents in roulette, twenty-five cents in craps. The bingo parlors, which are conspicuously absent in most of the big hotels, are here as are the keno games. Everywhere the emphasis is on big-payoff/poor-percentage games, on get-rich-quick. The action is directed toward the inveterate gamblers, sometimes even toward the addict. It is in these places that one is most likely to see the plungers who have long ago stopped having fun, those who spend whole days riveted to the slots, tugging absently at the levers, unmoved by payoff or loss, lulled into that peculiar gambler's stupor by the ecstatic rhythms of the machine.

Once the traveler to Vegas officially passes the pearly gates of a typical gambling hall, he finds himself transported to the center of an American fantasy. Everything here is the biggest, the fanciest, all unabashedly overdone, intentionally gaudy. The rugs are ridiculously thick. The chandeliers are too large. The dealer is wearing a cowboy suit or tails. The shills are dressed like Buf-

For some obscure psychological reason, gamblers love to operate in small, jampacked area. Las Vegas obliges by jumbling casinos, night clubs, hotels, restaurants, and other life-support systems together on one short neon-lit avenue.

falo Bill. Look at the enormous dollar sign engraved in the mirror behind the bar. The casino proudly tells you it's the largest of its kind in the world.

Money passes hands as in a Monopoly game. There is smoke in the air, there are cries of excitement, there is sex. Everyone is acting rich, and the housemen urge them on. It seems the whole environment is conspiring to alter the nine-to-five reality, to replace it with a million-dollar surrogate and then convince the patron that this is what life is *really* all about, that tonight he too is a giant, able to afford those reckless flings which previously he has only experienced in his fantasies. The message is subliminally transmitted through the schema of things: "Enjoy yourself," "Let go," "Anything can happen and just might," "It *can* happen to you," "Spend, spend, spend!"

Yet behind the beguiling façade lurks another side of things, the paranoid and uneasy world of casino management. The rule in Vegas is that everybody watches everybody, and this is not only for reasons of glamour but because the specter of cheating haunts the atmosphere. This is why the walls of many casinos are lined with mirrors. The mirrors are really one-way glass. Behind them stand lookouts alert for cheaters on the take.

Guards are a prerequisite here. They can be seen making the rounds from room to room, or standing ominously by the doors like wooden Indians. Scores of plainclothesmen join them, mixing at the tables, while closed-circuit television watchers scan the floor. Precautions generally prove effective. But then comes the next question: who guards the guards? Employee cheating has become something of an epidemic in Vegas in the past few years. Applicants for casino work today are fingerprinted, and anyone with a prison record is disqualified. Female employees are not allowed to carry purses on the job or to wear clothes with large pleats. Dealers—male or female—may not place their hands in their pockets, and if necessity makes this imperative there is a prescribed way it must be done: hands are slipped into the pockets with fingers straight, brought out with outstretched palms, and turned over twice. Several years ago an incident took place in a casino that made this extra turn necessary. It was found that one dextrous dealer had learned to palm bills backhand, in the manner of a stage magician.

Puerto Rico

If you are used to doing your gambling in Nevada, you are in for a few surprises the first time you try a Puerto Rican casino. First of all, if you get there too early you will find it closed. Unlike Las Vegas, which provides 'round-the-clock action, most Puerto Rican clubs open at 8 p.m. and close at 4 a.m. Even if the casino is open, you won't get in unless you are wearing a tie and jacket. This is a requirement in all casinos on the island. It's even rougher for the dealers—they have to wear tuxedos. Once inside, don't expect to be able to relax with a drink while you play. Alcohol is forbidden in the game rooms by the Department of Tourism, which strictly regulates all casino gambling on the island.

There are more than a dozen casinos in and around San Juan, the most popular being El San Juan, the Americana, the Dorado del Mar, the Dorado Beach Hotel, and El Conquistador. Although the clubs differ in size and splendor, they all offer the same games run in the same manner. (This uniformity is also due to government regulation.) In all of the casinos you can play craps, blackjack, and roulette. Some also offer baccarat, and slot machines have recently been introduced.

The games are conducted as they are in Las Vegas, but with a few differences. Carefully watch those differences. In craps, place bets on 6 and 8 are paid off at even money rather than Vegas odds of 7 to 6, making this a sucker bet to be avoided. Blackjack is dealt face up from a shoe and players may only double down on a count of 11. This may seem like a minor restriction to the casual player, but serious blackjack players consider Puerto Rico just about the worst place in the world to play the game because of it. Roulette is played with an American wheel, as in Nevada, which means there is a zero and a double zero to cut down the player's chances. All games are played with a one-dollar minimum.

London

After more than a century during which most forms of gambling were prohibited, casino gambling was legalized in England in 1960. Within a few years there were more than 2,500 gambling houses in the country and abuses were widespread. Sweeping reforms were adopted in 1970 and since then London has become one of the best places in the world to play.

The clubs in London are subdued and posh, and the atmosphere is sedate. This is partially due to the fact that no alcoholic beverages are allowed in the gaming rooms and the bars close at midnight. The elegance is ensured by a requirement that gentlemen wear jackets, and in some clubs, ties.

Casino gambling is only permitted in private clubs. That means you must first become a member of the club in which you want to play. About the only requirement for membership is that you pay a fee, usually about $10 to $25. However, there is a government-imposed waiting period of 48 hours (to eliminate impulse gaming) between the time a visitor registers at a club and the time he can begin playing. Keep this in mind and register at the clubs where you wish to play as soon as you arrive in London. Registration is good for life. You can get around both the waiting period and registration fee if you go as the guest of any member of the club who has already qualified under the "48-hour" rule.

English clubs like to claim that they offer the best odds in the world. Generally, they're right. In craps, they pay 9½ to 5 on place bets on 4 and 10 rather than the 9 to 5 paid in Las Vegas. They offer a more liberal Field than do the Strip casinos in Vegas and also give better odds on many proposition bets while other propositions have been eliminated entirely. But keep in mind that even with the improved payoffs, propositions are still strictly sucker bets. In roulette they use European wheels, which have a single zero but no double zero, thus cutting the house edge almost in half. In addition, on even-money bets you get back half your wager when zero turns up.

Blackjack is one game where the player is not given any special break. The games are dealt face up from a shoe. Players may only double on 9, 10, or 11. They may split any pair except 4s, 5s, or 10s. They may double down after a split (except when splitting aces) but may not split again after a split. Insurance may be taken only by players who have been dealt naturals. There is no surrender option.

One concession to the novice blackjack player is the government regulation requiring the posting of suggested blackjack strategy. This is listed on a small card displayed on each table. This strategy is not as effective as the basic strategy given earlier in the book, but it is better than playing blindly. If you get confused you can always fall back on it.

Don't be surprised if someone stands behind you and bets on your blackjack hand. This is permissible and fairly common. But, of course, the player seated at the

Nassau: A pleasant blackjack dealer—like this one at lavish El Casino in Freeport—will help make winning more fun, losing slightly less painful. Roulette at Paradise Island Casino has different-colored chips for each player, thereby reducing arguments—and petty chiseling.

table still makes the strategic decisions. Another feature that might throw you at first is the fact that the dealer does not give himself a hole card until after all the players have played their hands. This improves the house's chances slightly.

Each club in London is only allowed two slot machines, and some clubs don't have any at all. You will also encounter a game called punto banco, which is only baccarat under a different title.

Dealers are forbidden by law to accept tips, and this is itself a break for the player. Casinos open at 2 p.m. and close at 4 a.m. Finally, remember that you are betting pounds, not dollars, Otherwise, you may end up deeper in the hole than you intended without realizing how it happened.

Monte Carlo

For the tourist-gambler in search of glamour and excitement there is the illustrious Casino de Monte Carlo in Monaco. It has become the most famous gambling center in Europe, and still benefits from the reputation it earned in the early part of the century as a favorite hangout of celebrities and royalty. Today, though the visitor is not likely to find as many stars or heads of state as there once were because in part of the proximity of French casinos, this fabulous resort continues to allure patrons.

The dignity and grandeur of the casino does not fail to impress even the most jaded travelers. It is a monument from a long-gone era, still trimmed with marble, mirrors, and crystal chandeliers. This building (now known as the Winter Casino) dominates the town, although a second casino (the Summer Casino) has recently been built. One of the casino's eleven rooms is called the "Kitchen," and here the amateurs and tourists generally gamble. It is in the *salles privées,* however,

where the wealthy international gambling set and big money are found.

The casino's staff is highly trained and rigidly disciplined to run the casino smoothly and efficiently. The casino maintains its own police force in addition to a security force. Croupiers must attend the casino's school for six to eight months, and must adhere to strict regulations in and out of the casino.

Some of the games available are blackjack (dealt from a six-deck shoe), craps (layout is different and may be confusing), roulette, chemin de fer, baccarat banque, trente et quarante (30-40), and slot machines (notoriously "tight"). The casino opens at 10 a.m. and closes at 2 a.m., and there is an admission charge at the door. There is no dress requirement during the day.

Nongamblers or visitors with spare time will find an overwhelming assortment of leisure activities: tennis tournaments, yachting regattas, skiing, ballets, operas, concerts, or just people-watching.

The Bahamas

There are two major casinos in the Bahamas. Both cater exclusively to tourists since local residents are prohibited by law from entering. El Casino in Freeport is a very large casino, lavishly furnished and beautifully designed in an Arabian Nights motif. It offers blackjack, craps, roulette, and hundreds of quarter slot machines. In blackjack you can double only on a count of 9, 10, or 11. You may split any pair but may not double after a split. All games are multiple deck.

The Paradise Island Casino is located just across the bridge from Nassau. It also offers blackjack (dealt from a shoe), roulette, craps, baccarat, and quarter slots. The blackjack rules are less favorable than in El Casino, allowing a double down only on a count of 11.

In both casinos, roulette is conducted exactly as in Nevada. All the crap tables in both clubs use the "New York" or "Eastern" layout. The casinos each have fine restaurants.

A third casino, although still on the drawing board, is bringing excitement to the Cable Beach area on Nassau. Playboy Clubs International, which operates four casinos in England, is favored to win the concession for operating the new casino and plans to introduce the better odds on all games now prevalent in Britain.

The Continent

When gambling in Europe you will, of course, encounter differences in procedures and in the games offered from one country to another and even from one casino to another within the same country. There are, however, certain features that most European casinos have in common and that will be new to those who are used to gambling in Nevada. First of all, they are not as easy to get into as American casinos. Most require tie and jacket and charge an admission fee. You will also usually be required to present your passport before being admitted.

The biggest differences in playing procedures are found in roulette. On the plus side there is the elimination of the double zero and the "en prison" feature. On the minus side is the fact that the games are usually dealt French-style. In American casinos each player is assigned a different color for his chips when he buys in at the table. That way there can be no question as to who bet on what. In the French manner of dealing roulette, all the players use chips of the same color. A group of gamblers spreading bets all over the layout is bound to lead to confusion and arguments. Such arguments are a common occurrence in European casinos. These are usually not civilized, restrained discussions but rather

World-famous Casino de Monte Carlo in Monaco glows warmly (opposite) and still attracts those looking for the glamour and excitement of an aristocratic resort. Bottom: Chips for every taste and bankroll. Below: Gambling for fun–not money–helps open Paris restaurant. Bottom r: Gambling as a social event.

screaming, jumping-up-and-down fights. Many result from honest error while others are the result of conscious dishonesty by petty cheats. The croupiers are the final arbiters in these disputes. If you find yourself in one of these quarrels with a local, you will be at an immediate disadvantage since the croupiers don't speak English and you probably don't speak whatever they are speaking.

In Europe, baccarat is called punto banco but despite the name change is played the same as in Las Vegas. Most casinos also offer baccarat banque and chemin de fer. The tables and layouts for these two games are very similar to that of baccarat, but the house percentage is greater in both. Be careful or you may accidentally sit down at the wrong game.

Two games found in Europe that have never reached American shores are French bank and trente et quarante. Both are simple to learn and enjoyable to play. Just watch the action for a little while to get the hang of them before you sit down to play.

How to Behave in the Casino

You're on your way to the Nevada casinos and you're not quite sure how to act once you get there. How to behave. How not to behave. Be of good cheer. The rules are few and easy to observe.

What to Wear

What to wear? The casinos in Europe, though not as formal as they were in the days of Victoria, still require, by and large, a minimum of coat and tie. If you like dressing up in evening clothes and putting on the dog then Monte Carlo is your place, as are some of the more chic English clubs or the private *cercles* in France.

However, if you're less formal, then come as you are to Nevada, where casual is the word. Comfortable clothes are all that is expected. If you want to dress up, fine; if you don't, that is fine too. Bring what you like and wear it.

When packing for a Las Vegas sojourn—which means you are from out of town, are going to be here for a few days, and probably are staying at a hotel—then make sure you bring appropriate evening wear. Entertainment is the be-all and end-all in this town, and if you want to wear your best this is the time to do it. Further, make certain you bring your swimsuit (every hotel has at least one pool), plus some cool clothes for the day and something to wrap up in at night (it's a desert climate— hot days, chilly nights), and some good walking shoes (you'll be on your feet a lot). Bring a pair of sunglasses, some shorts, and plenty of suntan lotion too.

Casino Deportment

Novice gamblers often wonder how to behave at the gambling table. They're confused in the beginning, not quite sure how to act and react. At some tables they find everyone is smiling and jovial. Players joke with the dealers as if they were old friends and everyone seems to be having a grand time. At other tables seriousness is the word: no chatting, no smiling, no nothing but pressures of the game. What *is* expected of one in such uncertain surroundings?

Generally the answer is to find the style of game you like and stick to it. If you're a no-nonsense man or woman, find a no-nonsense table. Though there are those times when a group of hyper-intense gamblers are grouped at one table with a hyper-intense dealer, croupier, or stickman as topping, most people play for fun just as much as they play for profit. This means the casino is by and large a cheerful place with plenty of sociability. Naturally there are certain rules of propriety one follows. These are few, largely unwritten, and good to know. Some of the basic ones are:

Be Careful about Kibitzing. First of all, it's rude. No one wants to be told how badly he's playing or how much better the kibitzer would play if he were holding the same hand. Second, it's bothersome to others. And third, at times it can be taken as a form of cheating. If a person is just watching a game he is expected to watch it without contributing his advice.

Talking while Playing. There is no hard, fast rule here. Certainly there are gregarious tables, even gregarious dealers, and certainly it's all right to make conversation in the course of a game. At the craps table there is always much noise and mirth—but craps has been a favorite of the noisemakers, and noisemakers usually make bad gamblers. Those who play by skill need to concentrate. This goes for you as well as the other guy. Too much chit-chat over the cards or dice is distracting. Mistakes are made, especially if playing a system. In the attempt to be overly sociable, a player can lose his or her concentration that is so vital to good gambling. So follow this rule—be friendly, be polite, but spend your real energies playing the game.

Be Careful of Liquor. This is an obvious rule but hard to follow, especially when the drinks are cheap or even on the house. But remember, even one ounce of alcohol impairs reflex and thought response by as much as 10 percent. Yes, even *one* drink. Nothing will affect a gambler's discretion faster than booze. So save it for after the game.

Lose Well, Win Well. Again, little need be said. A bad loser is not an infrequent sight in the Nevada casinos and, really, he or she is one of the most boring. Only adults are allowed to gamble and this for a sound reason: an adult is expected to be fully aware of the risks involved in chancing his money. If he loses, it is totally his responsibility, just as it is his responsibility not to throw tantrums or accusations if he comes out on the short end.

The same can be said about winning: nothing is as annoying as the gambler who crows his victory. Win or lose, it's best to remember that when one gambles he has an obligation to the other players—and one of these obligations is to accept his fate with dignity.

The Dealer: Your Friendly Enemy

Another problem players often face is how to relate to the dealer. As mentioned above, there are friendly dealers and unfriendly dealers. Really, dealers are just people. Players tend to project their fears or authority hang-ups onto the man who runs the game, and this is accompanied by unnecessary fantasy and paranoia. The dealer is just someone trying to make a living. He's fast with cards, maybe went to dealer's school, has kids, pays taxes, and has as many headaches as the rest of us. To make him bigger than life is an unfortunate mistake, just as thinking he's out to get *you* is utter foolishness.

In other words, the way to deal with the dealer is to think of him as an employee of a casino, one who is given a good salary to play his best against all comers. He does not, for the most part, act on a personal basis, and if by chance it becomes apparent that he does, one only has to move to another table.

If the dealer is friendly, be friendly back. There are many gamblers in Las Vegas who return time and again to the same table, not only because they think it's lucky but because they enjoy the dealer. If you find a dealer you like, stick with him. But remember, no matter how affable or accommodating he seems, he's still on payroll to the house, which means he's still out to beat you as often and as soundly as he can.

Cheating: You and Them

There is great diversity of opinion about the amount of cheating that takes place in Nevada. Some claim the crooked game is a thing of the past that belongs to the Gold Rush days, and also that the casinos can't afford the horrific publicity such scandal would bring. People call attention to the Nevada Gaming Control Board, which keeps a close monitor on the casinos and which comes down with an iron hand on any casino caught defrauding the public. Another school of thought on the subject believes that there's a lot more going on than anyone might expect in Nevada, and that institutions like the Gaming Control Board are ineffectual. They point to the notion that both Reno and Vegas are largely controlled by criminal syndicates and that cheating in Nevada is and always has been a way of life.

The truth no doubt lies somewhere in between. Cheating is far from exterminated in Nevada, and will never be exterminated there or anywhere else where gamblers convene. Yet by and large the casinos seem to be pretty clean. Gambling has become a corporate business in Nevada and it's all to executive interests to keep things above-board. The club owners get high profits with clean play, so why rock the boat? Not that they're such moral or ethical souls. It's just that they know that if out-of-towners have the slightest question concerning a casino's integrity they'll steer clear and bring their business elsewhere. The few dollars that might be picked up on a rigged apparatus or underhanded play is simply not worth the destruction a bad reputation would bring.

Nevertheless this does not mean that *all* Nevada gambling establishments are pearly white. A few aren't. How to tell? As a good rule of thumb, it's best to stick with the better-known places, the tried and true. If there's going to be cheating, it's more likely to occur in the down-and-out sections of town. Moreover, it will happen in places that don't have much to lose by surrendering their gambling permits. The one-armed bandit at the local liquor store is more likely to be gaffed than the ones at the Flamingo. The crap table at a dive is more likely to use false dice than those along the Strip.

If you are in a casino and you think you are being cheated, what then? First of all, *be sure*. Many people raise a large squall and come out looking sheepish when their accusations are discredited. If you're *sure* that something is going on, go to the manager or the pit boss and report it. Chances are he's as interested in learning about cheaters as you. Remember that dealers are simply hired hands. Occasionally some kind of prior agreement between patron and dealer does take place. Or sometimes the dealer simply wants to pocket a few extra bucks for himself. Whatever the case, the manager is eager to know about this and is well aware that his casino could lose its license if caught. All cheating should be reported to those in charge; one can be reasonably certain that action will be sure and swift.

Enjoy Yourself

If you've come to Nevada you've come for a good time. You'll find that the hotels, the motels, the casinos, the whole city itself is set up to accommodate you. There's everything for everybody here—or almost so—and really, this has got to be one of the easiest places in the world to have a good time. So go ahead, enjoy!

Casino Games

Within the casino the most popular of all amusements is the slot machine. The wheels and gears of these chromium idols whirr ceaselessly day and night (most casinos are open twenty-four hours a day) and stop only a minute

Ailing Mills Indian chief is trundled off for repairs. He is a product of the world's largest manufacturer of slots. He eats nickels and pays off a maximum "Special Award" of $10 —how frequently depending on greed of his operator. Nickel level is a good place for tyro to start.

Player Loss in One Hour*	
Game	*Loss per Hour*
Craps (pass, don't pass)	$ 9
Blackjack	$ 40
Roulette	$ 53
Chuck-a-luck	$ 78
Craps (field)	$111
Craps (2 or 12)	$333

betting $10 each time

each year, at twelve o'clock on New Year's Eve.

Next in popularity are the standard casino games: craps, twenty-one, roulette, and baccarat, in that order. Then follow chuck-a-luck, keno, bingo, the wheel of fortune, big six, and the lesser amusements, most of which are primarily played in the downtown clubs. Here are a few statistics you may want to know before you choose your game at the casino:

House Advantage	
Game	*House Percentage*
Blackjack	A "good" player can gain a .1% advantage over the house, an expert a 2.3% advantage.
Chuck-a-luck	8% and up
Slot machines	from 25% to 70%
Roulette	5.26% (except for the 5-number bet, which is 7.89%)
Baccarat	1.27% and up (sometimes lower)
Wheel of fortune	11.1% to 24%
Faro	2.0 and lower in certain bets
Craps	ranges from .59% to 16.5%, depending on bet

We have already taken a look at craps, blackjack, baccarat, and faro. We will shortly investigate roulette and bookmaking. Now it is time to meet the minor games, the big-jackpot, bad-odds amusements that are known among casino owners as "bread-and-butters."

The Slot Machine

The most seductive and most devastating gambling apparatus is the slot, the one-armed bandit. Invented in 1895 by a San Francisco mechanic named Charles Fey, the original machine was called the "Liberty Bell" and was placed on bar counters across the city. If the right combinations came up, players were paid off in drinks.

No patent can be taken out on a gambling machine, Fey learned, so to protect his interests in this promising enterprise he gained control of all distribution rights. Soon business was booming. A number of models rapidly emerged from his shop, most of them now paying off in silver rather than alcohol. Soon every bar had its machine. To old-timers the names of these turn-of-the-century inventions are still familiar: On the Square, Royal Jumbo, Silver Cup, Ben Franklin, Little Monte Carlo, The Dewey, and dozens more.

*Slots can exert addictive fascination for players,
some of whom seem as unmoved by winning as
by losing. Odds are never generous, but are best
at casinos. If you don't get a jackpot in
eight or ten tries, find a better machine. Slot
next to good machine probably won't be.*

For some years Fey enjoyed a monopoly of the market. The bubble burst when a shrewd Chicago businessman named Herbert Stephen Mills horned in on the action and began producing similar machines. Fey retired a rich man. Mills went on to become the largest manufacturer of slot machines in the world.

No other invention in history has ever made so much money for so small an investment as Fey's magic metal box. Not only did it grind the customer down with the inexorability that could only belong to a mathematically programmed instrument, but it did so by using the sucker's own muscle to turn the wheel. Here was the perfect study in perpetual motion: the customer paid for the right to provide the motive power for his own fleecing. No dealer, stickman, or shill was required. Before long the slot was a standard piece of equipment in every gambling house, and it soon became responsible for a sizable part of the house's net proceeds. In 1960, 40 million of the 200 million gambling dollars made in Nevada came from the slot business, making the bandit responsible for a fifth of all revenues. No wonder every club in Vegas today has its lineup of slot machines at the door, as does every laundromat, beauty shop, and supermarket.

(Here, incidentally, a word to the wise: when in Nevada beware of slot machines outside the casino. The casino percentages are bad enough. Even the "loose" machines take 10 to 20 percent for the house. In the carwash and drug store, however, the slots sometimes are set to keep as much as 80 and 90 percent, true banditry. There are no regulations in Nevada as to how high earnings can be on these mechanical money-eaters, nor is there any way of determining what the odds and profit factors are by looking at them.)

Can the one-armed bandit be beaten? Almost never. True, at different times it has been bested by cheaters (using magnets, drilling holes in the side plates and slipping wires into the ring mechanism, dropping slugs, jamming rods up the payoff tube), and by manipulators (the somewhat successful "rhythm" players of several years ago devised an intricately timed system of pulling and releasing the lever in synchronization with the turning of the inner governor mechanism), but in the past few years casino mechanics have modified the instrument to the point where it is not only jimmy-proof, but impervious to any outside shock short of a cobalt bomb.

From a serious gambler's standpoint, the odds in a slot machine are ridiculous. On a three-reel mechanism the number of possible combinations is 8,000. On the four-reel there are 64 million combinations. Yet how few of these combinations pay off. Some machines are set at better percentages than others, but none of them is anything to boast about. Why then do people play? First, because the slot is easy. It requires no skill or reason. Second, because the uninformed player has no notion of just how prohibitively the odds are stacked against him. Third, because the slots are the perfect solitary amusement, the ideal entertainment for those frightened by the big action at the tables. Fourth, because the clink and hum and flash and blur of the one-armed bandit exerts a far stronger hypnotic action on the human mind than anyone has yet imagined. And fifth, because it's fun.

So if you are going to play the slots—and how many of us can resist a pull or two?—do it in the best of possible ways. First, make sure you play the nickel and quarter machines. Generally they offer the best payoff rates. Also, set a limit on losses and resist the mesmerizing inner call of "just one more coin." Don't make the mistake of thinking that all machines are alike. Some are programmed to pay off high, some low. In downtown Las Vegas many casinos pride themselves on their liberal

slots, and on the fact that their machines work at a low— for the slots—return of 90 cents to the dollar. (Compare that to the 0.55 percent house advantage at certain bets in craps and you will see why slot players die broke.) Make sure you locate a machine set at reasonable odds. If a slot does not pay a jackpot after eight, or at most ten, tries, you can be pretty sure it is a lemon. Once you've found your pet machine, stick with it. Do *not* play the machines positioned near it. Why? Because many players like to work several slots at a time. Knowing this, the management places poor payers next to the richer ones in hopes that the high percentages will reimburse them for the low.

Systems? There have been a few, though none that have brought their creators much gain. A favorite is to start on the nickel machines with a prescribed amount of capital. If you get a payoff before you pass the established limit (staying within the limit is what is most crucial), you take your winnings and sink them into the quarter machine. Another payoff, and on to the 50-cent slot, still another and you try the dollar. This way, if you set a limit to your losses and gamble only when you are hitting jackpots, you will always be playing with the house's money. As any gambler will tell you, this is the way to gamble.

Bingo

When the nongambler learns that bingo is a gambling game his response is often surprise and even amusement. Bingo is a children's game, something played at Rotary Club benefits and church bazaars! Isn't it?

Those from Las Vegas see bingo in a different light. They are well aware that it is more than hometown fun, that it is a $2 billion-a-year enterprise, a controversial gambler's sport, the legality of which has caused much bitter debate, and the proceeds from which have helped

finance schools, churches, and underworld empires.

And yet it *is* a picturesque and gentle game. Derived from lotto, which in turn was taken from the principles of the ancient Italian National Lottery, bingo's attraction lies in its sweet simplicity. After paying what is usually a modest admission at the door, the player purchases cards on which twenty-five random numbers from 1 to 75 are arranged in five columns. The player may buy as many cards as he is capable of playing (a bingoist manning as many as twenty cards is not an unusual sight in the casinos). In front of the bingo room is a large cage holding seventy-five numbered balls. When everyone is seated and the game begins, these balls are drawn one at a time by the bingo operator and given to the "caller" to announce. Each time one of these numbers corresponds to a number on the player's card the player covers it with a marker. When a player covers all the numbers in one of his vertical, horizontal, or diagonal rows he shouts, "Bingo!" If all the numbers check, he wins a money prize, which in Nevada can vary from $20 to $5,000.

Many people love this game. The costs of playing are small; reports have it that the average amount spent for an evening of bingo is about $6.50. Someone always wins, and the illusion that the player has "just missed" getting a bingo each game makes it all quite suspenseful and fun. Popularity notwithstanding, bingo is considered a bit of an annoyance among casino owners. It is not commonly found along the Strip and is tolerated downtown, where the managers complain that space taken up by 25-cent bettors could house high-priced games. Actually, the real reason bingo has traditionally been tolerated is because it gives wives something to do while their husbands are out losing their shirts at craps or twenty-one. This image is now a bit dated; in the 1970s wives may be losing their shirts along with their husbands'. Still, any afternoon peep into the bingo parlor will prove that bingo belongs primarily to the ladies.

A Tip for Bingo Players. One fallacy about bingo should be cleared up once and forever. Many people believe that by playing several cards at once their chances of winning are increased. Mathematically this does not hold true. For although it is true that the chances of winning are approximately ten times greater, the price that must be paid by the player increases tenfold but the amount he may win does not increase. Hence, there is no net percentage gain. So save your money and play the single card.

Keno

The original keno, really just a version of bingo, has in the past years been thoroughly supplanted by "racehorse keno," a game descended from the Chinese lottery and introduced to western America by Oriental railroad laborers in the nineteenth century.

Like bingo, keno is a low-investment, low-return gamble. Winnings are scarce. The house grabs an 18 to 25 percent edge. For obvious reasons, keno is popular with casino owners; yet many gamblers love it too, gener-

Neon signs, flashing arrows, colossal marquees, and all kinds of eye-catching phantasma are designed to attract the Las Vegas trade. Bingo parlors, keno games, penny slot machines, and big-payoff/low-percentage games directed toward the inveterate gambler are concentrated downtown in Casino Center.

ally for the same reasons they like bingo, but also because it offers the chance to win a grand prize of $25,000—which is offered at the interesting odds of 9 million to one.

To play keno, a kenoist must purchase his card directly from the counter in front of the room. On this card are listed the numbers 1 through 80. Players mark one to fifteen of the numbers, write in the amount of their wager, hand in the bets, receive a receipt from the window, and then await the result of the drawing which is made by plucking twenty out of eighty numbered table-tennis balls from a large, transparent bowl called a

Keno Statistics		
Ticket	*Payoff*	*House Edge*
One-spot ticket	Pays $3.20 for $1 bet	20%
Two-spot ticket	Pays $13 for $1	21%
Three-spot ticket	Catch two numbers get money back	26%
	Catch three numbers pays $47 for $1	
Four-spot ticket	Catch two numbers get money back	24%
	Catch three numbers pays $47 for $1	
	Catch four numbers pays $118 for $1	
Five-spot ticket	Catch three numbers pays $3 for $1	21%
	Catch four numbers pays $26 for $1	
	Catch five numbers pays $332 for $1	

the electronic keno board. If enough of the numbers marked on a player's card agree with those picked from the goose the player will collect—how much depending on the type of bet he has riding and the number of winning numbers he has chosen.

For example, on the "one-spot ticket" the player bets a single number, 1 through 80. If the number is picked during the drawing he wins. Twenty tries to make one number sounds fair enough. But remember, it is not twenty numbers but eighty. This makes it a 3 to 1 deal, twenty tries out of eighty possibilities, with the payoff only 2.2 to 1. The ticket actually pays $3.20 for a $1.00 investment, but remember that the house keeps the player's $1.00 whether he wins or loses. That's the rub. Similarly, on a "two-spot ticket" the player bets on two numbers, and if he wins he gets a payoff appropriately increased from the one-spot ticket. The spot tickets go up to 15, and the big jackpots come when the bettor correctly chooses from ten to fifteen spots on a $2.50 ticket. Innumerable other types of bets are also made at keno. But they are just variations on the basic method, which ultimately boils down to a numbers game.

In Las Vegas, keno is thought to be something of an intermission, a chance to rest and fritter away a few dollars between gladiatorial bouts at the heavier amusements. Indeed, the keno lounge, or the area thereabouts, is often filled with such soft chairs, such accessible bars, and so many attractive female runners available to do all the betting work, that it is usually the most comfortable, if not the most profitable, place in the whole casino.

Chuck-a-luck

Chuck-a-luck, or birdcage as some people call it, was once quite popular among a segment of the dice-rolling population until craps came along and swept it into the wings.

Text continued on page 225

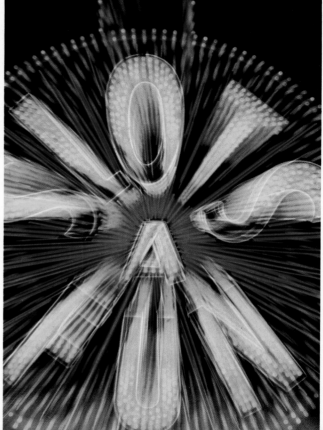

Lining the famous Strip in Las Vegas are eighteen mammoth hotels, each with its own casino, night club entertainment, and restaurants. There are some one hundred thousand rooms always available. Hotels generally pamper their guests, knowing that the longer they stay, the more they'll gamble.

Top: Inside the casino the decor is luxurious.
The effect is to treat patrons like millionaires, so they
will spend like them. Right: Multicolored stacks
of chips look like a child's play money, but can wipe out the life
savings of anyone who treats them as such. Baccarat
(above) and roulette (opposite) have "snob appeal."

Left: To help prevent employee cheating, dealers may not place their hands in pockets and females may not wear pleated skirts. Below: Slot machines in Nevada's casinos are considered the "loosest" in the world. Opposite: Dreams of hitting the jackpot encourage coin after coin. The actual chance of a jackpot, or here a triple bar, is 1 in 2,667.

Today it is still played, not much, but enough to justify its existence. Most of its patrons are greenhorns taken in by the simplicity of the rules and by the pitchman's logic of "three winners and three losers every time."

Here is the way it works. The layout shows the numbers 1 through 6, and players put their bets on any of these numbers. Three dice are shaken up in an hourglass-shaped cage. If the player's number appears on one of the three dice he wins and is paid off at even money. If his number appears on two of the dice the payoff is at 2 to 1, and if on three it is 3 to 1, all very fair. But let's look more closely. Suppose each of the six squares is covered with bets of a dollar. The numbers 2, 5, and 6 show up on the three dice and each player gets $2 back. Fine. Next roll two 3s and a 5 appear. Now the player betting the 3 receives his double payoff, $3, the player betting the 5 gets his $2. Only $5 has been paid out of the $6 bet, with the house keeping the extra $1. And if three 3s should appear the house will pay out only $4 (3 to 1 to one player only), keeping $2 and making the house advantage in this case a rollicking 40 percent. In most people's opinions chuck-a-luck is more a game of the carnival than of the casino. The only ones who disagree are those who run the casinos.

Big Six

Big six is more or less chuck-a-luck on a wheel. The most common type of wheel—there are some with different designs that have even higher house percentages—is an ornate, eight-foot-high carnival wheel with a Masonic-looking star in the center. The rim of the wheel is apportioned into fifty-four equal sections, each showing a different possible combination of three dice. The wheel is spun. The players put their bets on the same type of six-number layout used in chuck-a-luck. If their number shows on the pictured dice when the wheel comes to a stop they win at the same schedule as in chuck-a-luck.

The big drawback with big six is that there are only six sections on this wheel which *do not* show a pair, twenty-four which *do* show pairs, and twenty-four with three pairs. Think about it. There are "three winners and three losers every time" only six times out of fifty-four. On all other spins one or two players come into the money while the rest win nothing at all. The house takes 22 percent. Might as well play the slots.

Wheel of Fortune

Like the big-six wheel, the wheel of fortune has variations in design and house percentage, depending on where you play. The most common stands about eight feet high and is divided into fifty-four sections. In fifty-two of these sections greenbacks are displayed under glass, ranging in denomination from $1 to $20. A flag and a joker fill the remaining slots. Players bet on which bills the indicator will point to when the wheel comes to a stop. The payoffs equal the value of the bill, i.e., winnings on $1 are at 1 to 1, on a five-dollar bill, 5 to 1, and so on, with the joker and the flag both paying 40 to 1. In downtown Vegas minimum bets are 25 cents, on the Strip a dollar. The general odds on the wheel's action look like this:

Bill	Payoff	Real Odds	House Edge
$1	1–1	53–24	11.1%
$2	2–1	53–15	16.7%
$5	5–1	53– 7	25.9%
$10	10–1	53– 4	18.0%
$20	20–1	52– 2	22.0%
flag	40–1	53– 1	24.0%
joker	40–1	53– 1	24.0%

Roulette

Of all gambling devices the one most reminiscent of that very fate which a gambler tempts is the wheel. In classical Greece the plunger used the wheel in his games of chance. So did the ancient Chinese, the Aztec, and the Eskimo. The symbol is universal. It makes us think of fate's wheel or the medieval wheel of destiny. It also makes us think of the famous kismet rondo, roulette.

Roulette: the very name conjures up associations of elegant rooms and mysterious countesses, James Bond, and Arabian sheiks—a game for the truly civilized, no doubt. This of course is fine. If you want to feel truly civilized, then play roulette. No one will hassle you in this corner of the casino, for here the activity is subdued and the atmosphere polite, nothing at all like the bedlam by the crap table. If you want to make a big killing though, better not stay at the roulette table for long. The high house percentage will finally grind you down.

Roulette rules are relatively easy to master. At first glance perhaps the willy-nilly way in which the chips are spread over the layout may perplex the newcomer, but it shouldn't, as the betting procedure is logical.

In roulette, several props are used:

1. A wooden wheel with the numbers 1 through 36, plus

a zero and double zero, embossed on the rim. The numbers are alternately red and black, the zeroes green.

2. A betting layout marked with the same numbers found on the wheel, plus several sections for side bets.

3. Columns of chips purchased from the house in packets of twenty, and ranging in value from 10 cents to $100.

The players place their chips on the chosen numbers. The croupier spins the wheel (there are several croupiers at a table in Europe, usually only one in Nevada). He drops the ball and calls out, "No more bets." If the ball then settles on the bettor's number he wins. His payoff is dependent on the type of wager he has made and the amount of money he has hazarded.

In roulette there is a pleasing variety of bets and it is this choice that makes the game so interesting. In the long run no one wager will pay any more than any other; the 5.26 percent house advantage is a constant in every bet but one. The thrill of winning at 35 to 1, however, is perhaps worth the excessive viggorish. Here are the bets that can be made:

One-number Bet. A chip is placed on a single number (including zero and double zero). If the number turns up on the next spin the bettor gets a payoff of 35 to 1.

Two-number Bet. This is made by placing a chip on the line which separates two numbers. If the ball lands on either of these two numbers the payoff is at 17 to 1.

High-low Number Bet. On the roulette layout you will see one section marked "1 to 18" and another marked "19 to 36." These are for the high and low bets. If a player puts his chips in the first section he wins if the next number that shows is from 1 to 18. If he puts his money on the second section, any of the numbers from 19 to 36 will bring him a payoff. In both cases, high and low, the payoff is at even money.

Even-odd Bet. When a player puts chips in the section

marked "odd," he will win at even money if an odd number turns up on the next roll. Even bets are placed in the section marked "even." The payoff is the same.

Red-black Bet. The same principle applies here as in the high-low and even-odd bets. The player puts his chips in the section marked "black." If a black-colored number appears he wins. To bet red he wagers his money in the "red" section. The payoff is at even money.

Three-number Bet. The player bets that one out of three chosen numbers will show. He makes it by placing the chip as indicated. The three-number bets earn 11 to 1.

Four-number Bet. These are placed as shown and pay 8 to 1.

Five-number Bet. If you must play the five-number bet, do so as shown below. But why bother? This is the only bet in the game where the usual 5.26 percent house advantage is raised, and raised to considerably more than 7 percent. This bet exists only to ensnare the uninformed. Ignore it.

Six-number Bet. This pays 5 to 1 and is placed as shown.

Twelve-number Column Bet. Here the player is actually buying one third of the numbers on the layout and betting that one of them will turn up on the next spin. In the column bet, the player puts his money in one of the compartments at the end of the layout marked "2 to 1." If any of the numbers included in the horizontal column adjacent to it wins he collects at 2 to 1.

Twelve-number Bet. The principle is the same as in the column bet, but now the chip is placed on one of the spaces marked either "1st 12" (the numbers 1–12), "2nd 12" (the numbers 13–24), or "3rd 12" (the numbers 25–36). If one of the numbers included in this bet shows up, the bettor collects at 2 to 1.

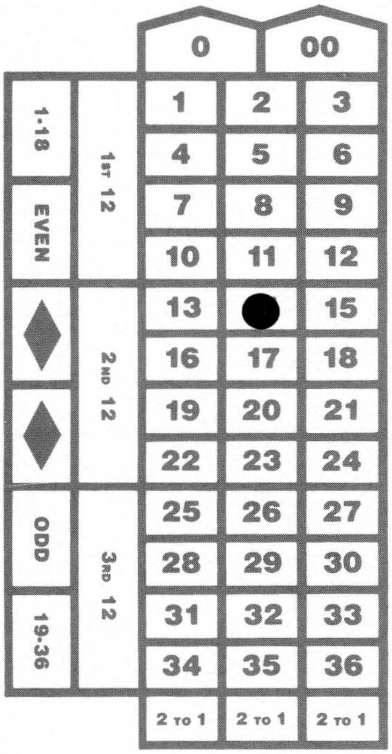

One-number Bet

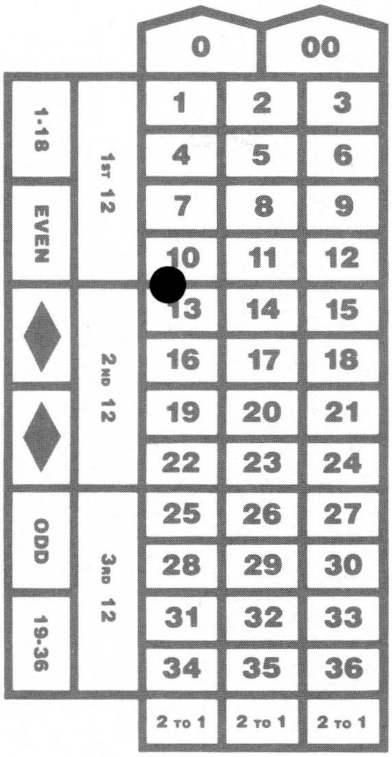

Two-number Bet

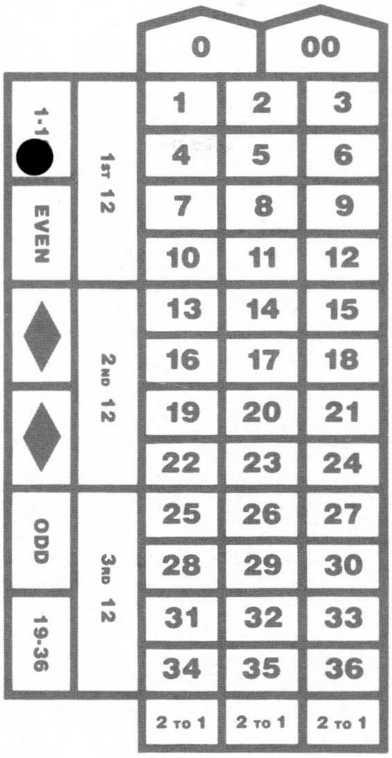

High-low number Bet

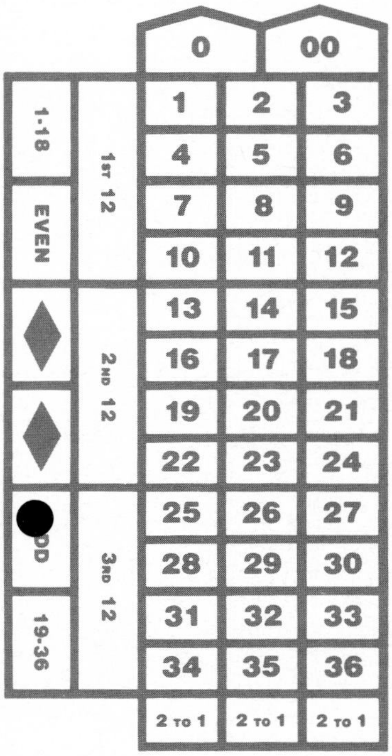

Even-odd Bet

Red-black Bet

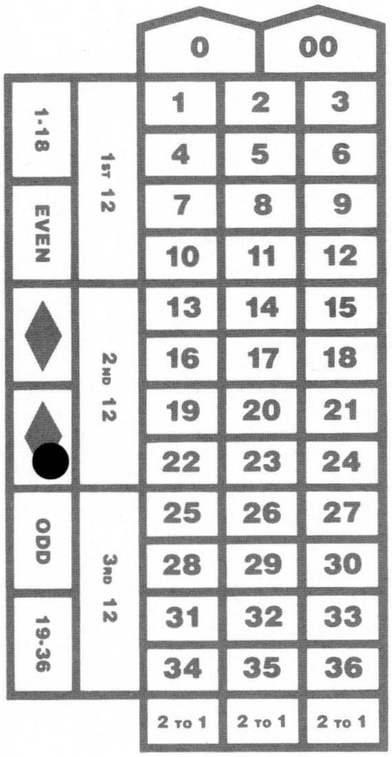

Three-number Bet

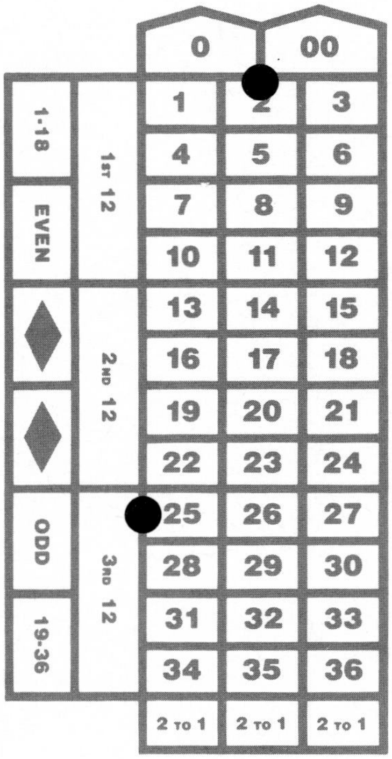

Four-number Bet

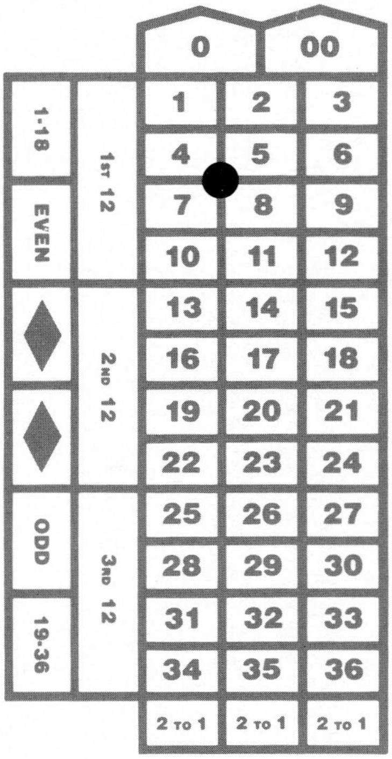

Five-number Bet

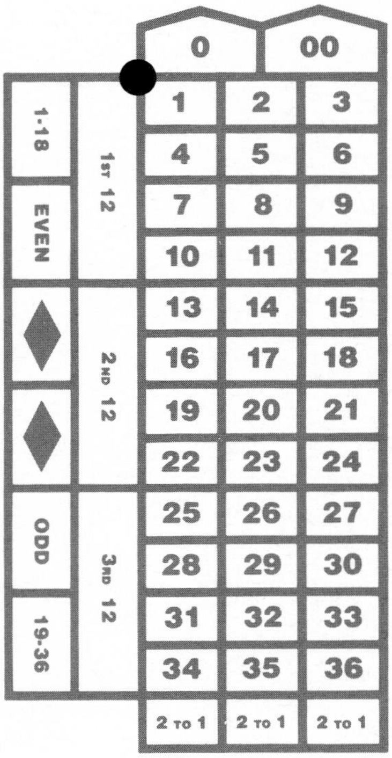

The origins of roulette are contradictory and indistinct. One theory claims that it was invented by the great French philosopher-mathematician Blaise Pascal, as a sort of by-product of his experiments with perpetual motion. Another, probably apocryphal, has it that the sport emerged from European monasteries where it was created to amuse the monks during their long winter retreats. The game as it is known in today's casinos is by no means old and seems to have come into general popularity around the turn of the eighteenth century, an offshoot of the still much-played game of boule. Though never terribly popular in America—the roulette table usually has the least traffic of all the big-money games in Nevada—Europeans still find it fascinating, and with good reason. Since 1840 their roulette wheel has shown a single zero only, reducing the house advantage on most bets to a reasonable 2.70 percent, and an even lower 1.35 percent on "en-prison" bets. En-prison bets work this way: when a zero is rolled, all bets placed on red-black, odd-even, or high-low are put to the side, "in prison," instead of being collected by the house. The wheel is spun again. If this time any of these bets wins, it is put back to its original position, "out of prison," and the player can do with it as he pleases, either removing it entirely from the table or letting it ride. Thus the player under the *en prison* rule loses only one half of his wager on all even-money bets.

Why American gambling establishments have not adopted the single-zero system is a mystery to many gamblers. Though some casinos experiment with it, most continue to maintain the American rules, and as a result roulette's popularity sinks lower year after year. Until something is changed, this trend will no doubt continue.

So the lesson is clear: play roulette in Nevada for fun, kicks, or for fantasy fulfillment, but don't play to break the bank.

Six-number Bet   **Twelve-number Column Bet**   **Twelve-number Bet**

231

*Casinos are traditional centers for bets
on all manner of sporting events, in U.S. most
particularly baseball. Long schedule,
many games per day in season, and every fan's
certainty that he can figure form make
baseball perhaps biggest sport for gamblers.*

Betting on Sports

It may seem peculiar to include sports betting in a section on the casinos, but the reasons for doing so are sound, first of all because only in Nevada is sports betting legal, and second because a vast majority of the best odds-makers just happen to reside in this bet-happy state.

Next to the horses, sports attracts more gambling dollars than any other game in America. Of all the betting sports, baseball is traditionally the most popular, especially around World Series time, when the usual $20,000 maximum bet ceiling is lifted. In the past few years, though, football has made rapid gains toward becoming the number-one American sport, and this swing has shown up on the bookie charts, too. In fact, one of the biggest events of the year for bookies is the Super Bowl. Estimates of the amount wagered for the 1975 game ranged as high as $260 million. Accurate statistics are hard to come by, of course, but by all accounts it seems that baseball gets approximately 45 percent of the action, football 40 percent. Basketball and hockey run a poor third and fourth, with about 15 percent of the business between them, and then a long train of lesser sports follows, among them golf, bowling, jai-alai, billiards, lacrosse, boxing, squash, tennis, soccer, track, and college wrestling.

There is argument over whether or not a bettor can make profits consistently betting on sports. Some experts call sports the best of all possible gambles, others pronounce it a dead end. The truth is that both sources are right and wrong; it just depends on which type of sports bet they are referring to.

For example, if a bookie gives a client what is known as the "40-cent line," then, yes, the bettor will be getting a raw deal. Working with the 40-cent line, if two teams are "pick 'em," that is, evenly matched, this means

that all bets should rightfully be at even money. Nonetheless your 40-cent-line bookie will offer odds at 7 to 5— seven dollars of your money to five of his.

Better, therefore, is the "20-cent line." Here the odds at pick 'em are something like, say, 6 to 5. This may not seem much of a change, but in fact that one point cuts radically into the book's profit and vastly increases the bettor's chances of gain. The trouble is that the 20-cent line usually can be wheedled out of a bookie only if you are a good customer, or if you come through with the big-money bets. It is also worth noting that there are 10-cent lines and 5-cent lines. But forget it. These are normally only for the trade.

Baseball

Traditionally, this offers bettors their greatest chance of success. Skillful betting in baseball depends on three factors. Most important is analysis of pitching. Then comes the general comparative strengths and weaknesses of teams. Finally, there is the question of whether a ball club is playing at home or away.

When evaluating a pitcher look for two things: his current won-and-lost record and his lifetime record against a particular club. If a pitcher has a losing record for the year, but a hefty winning lifetime average over the team he is throwing against, bet on him. He is probably a nemesis to the hitters on that club. If opposing pitchers are evenly matched, bet on the pitcher who is working in his home stadium.

In baseball the general rule is that the better teams usually beat the poorer teams. There are many exceptions, and these often turn on the oddest and least likely factors. It is here that knowledge and inside information become so essential. The average bettor, the guy on the street, has no chance of competing with the bookie's

octopuslike network of data feedback. Not only do the bookies have hourly sports-line information pumped into their offices by hired handicappers from Vegas and elsewhere, but they constantly seek to establish inside sources among the ballplayers themselves. Facts are continually pouring in concerning sore arms, changes in the line-up, rumors of a trade, births or deaths in a family, arguments in the locker rooms. The intimacy of it all is astonishing, and, indeed, the manner in which sports figures are watched by the betting world is a little-known sidelight of the professional athlete's private life.

Every bit of this information, no matter how trifling, may be of importance. In St. Louis a star pitcher once got himself stone drunk the night before a big game. The news of his inebriation was instantly known to every bookie in town, yet this fact alone did nothing to change the odds, as this particular twirler was famous for his ability to pitch well even under the cloud of a hangover. That night, however, the player's wife called up and bawled him out for his indiscretion. Bang! The odds against St. Louis increased all over the city. (It is a known fact that players play poor baseball when their wives are angry with them.) The following morning, though, the odds had returned to their original position. A spy sent from a bookie's office had read a telegram in the hotel lobby from the pitcher's wife, forgiving him.

No single person can compete with such far-reaching scrutiny, which, along with the loaded odds, is what gives the bookie his edge. Still, the well-informed sports bettor has a vast advantage over the shot-in-the-darker. The rule therefore is simple: the more you know about the teams you are betting on, the better your chances are for figuring winners.

Here are some other points of importance for baseball bettors:

Basketball, like football, is bet on point spreads, which are affected by such unfathomable factors as hot streaks, road fatigue, key players fouling out. One almost sure thing, however, is the home-court advantage.

1. Don't let partisanship stand in your way. You may be a Giant fan. But this shouldn't stop you from betting on the Dodgers if you find them the superior team. Sentiment has no place in the gambler's world.

2. Go to every game you can. Get hold of all the information available. Make yourself an expert before you bet.

3. Try this experiment: make a number of dry-run bets before you actually plunk down your cash. See what your win/lose percentage is in these dress rehearsals. Only when you are satisfied with the results of this experiment should you hazard real green.

4. Look for hot streaks among ballplayers and among teams. A hot streak in sports is just as worthy of a bet as a hot streak in craps. Also, the same is true in reverse: steer away from losing streaks and cold ballplayers.

5. Major-league teams are usually pretty well matched. Nonetheless, smart money usually bets the favorite. Percentage-wise, good teams usually come out on top, and a bet on the underdog doesn't usually pay that much more, anyway.

6. Confine your bets to two or three ball clubs. It will be difficult enough to amass significant statistics on these few teams. Trying to dope out the entire major leagues is something even the big timers find difficult. Specialize.

Football

In football, point spreads rather than odds are what count. For example, if Notre Dame is a 6½-point favorite over Iowa (the half point is to avoid ties), this means the Irish must win by 7 *points or better* in order to pay off. A win of 6 points or less is a loser. In football, therefore, the team with the higher score is not always the winner at the bookie's office.

There is another difference between baseball and football. Whereas most baseball bets are placed on major-

league teams, the action in football is equally divided between college and the pros. Those who bet the college teams look for a number of indications: what kind of physical shape is a team in? Is the game home or away? (For reasons no one can explain, teams win their *second* home game with a consistency far greater than the law of averages should allow, and as a result several football betting systems are built upon this fact alone.) What are the emotional factors surrounding a game? Is it a grudge match, with one team straining at the leash to avenge itself for last year's trouncing, or is it just a warm-up for a much bigger game the following week? There are the more pedestrian considerations, too: won/lost records, condition of star players, winning or losing streaks, number of yards given up by the defense, rushing averages, etc.

In pro football the teams are more evenly matched. The emphasis therefore is on individual positions, especially on the quarterback. If a quarterback has been moving his team lately, bet on him. Also quarterbacks just traded are worth keeping an eye on. Traded players often get hot the minute they join a new club. The statistical factors must be taken into consideration, especially defensive records (in many ways pro football has become predominantly a defensive game), rushing and passing averages, plus all the rest. As in baseball the key is *how much you know* about the teams involved.

Basketball

The point-spread system is also employed in basketball, as is the college-pro split. Basketball is not popular among bettors, though. First, the game is characterized by too many erratic point spreads. Second, there are many unpredictable factors, such as referee partisanship, road fatigue, unaccountable hot and cold streaks, foul-outs by key players, and so on. And third, because basketball is still

tainted with a reputation for crookedness earned during several famous "point-shaving" and "dumping" scandals some years ago.

Generally speaking, those who do bet this game look for the following things:

1. Whether a team is playing at home or away. More than any other sport, the home team in basketball has the advantage.

2. Comparative height. The taller team has the advantage.

3. Comparative field-goal and free-throw percentages.

4. Physical shape. A team that has just returned from a long road trip is usually a tired team.

The Private Bet

A parting look at the world of betting possibilities brings us out of the sphere of the casino and into that of the personal, one-on-one wager. Since the dawn of time men have been willing to hazard their teeth on just about anything: the number of minutes a chicken will last against a bear; the distance from here to the asteroids; how many angels can dance on the head of a pin . . . anything. We know, for example, that Count Buckenburg, a German author, once bet (and won) that he could ride from London to Edinburgh sitting backward on his horse. George, Lord Oxford (called Mad Lord George for the fact that he rode through London in a chariot pulled by three reindeer) bet another nobleman that a drove of geese would beat an equal number of turkeys in a race from Norwich to London. Which flock was the winner we do not know, although it has been recorded that when the Duke of Chartres wagered Count Fenlis that the latter could not ride from Paris to Fontainebleau and back in the time it took the Duke to prick five hundred thousand holes in a piece of paper, the good Count was victorious.

Thomas "Jerusalem" Wholly, another high roller, gained his strange nickname through a spur-of-the-moment challenge. While he was sitting comfortably one day in his private club in London, a friend bet him that he would not have the nerve to go downstairs, saddle his horse, and ride directly to the city of Jerusalem without even returning home for a change of clothes. Mr. Wholly accepted the bet on impulse and galloped off the moment the agreement was signed. He returned a year later and collected £15,000, a huge amount for his time.

A Few Standard Bets

Some people, it seems, will bet on anything. Nonetheless there are certain types of head-on bets that through the years have become standards. Usually these bets are to the point, easily performed, and quickly decided. They can be made in a barroom, at sporting events, in the living room, any place where people congregate. Some of the most popular bets of this kind are:

The Flip of a Coin. Whenever a final authority is needed, a coin will be produced, perhaps because a flip is particularly simple and decisive. The bettor wagers which side of a coin will turn up on the next toss—winner take all. Gamblers who want to get to the point find this a wonderful means of fast-money turnover, and often the flipping becomes a game in itself. (Beware of double-faced coins.)

The Cut of the Cards. This bet is as quick as the coin

flip, provided one happens to have a pack of cards handy. Opponents cut for the highest card (or occasionally the lowest) with the single cut determining the outcome. This type of bet is often used as a last-chance wager ending a night's game of cards. The big winner agrees to cut the cards with the big loser for double-or-nothing. Watch out for card sharks.

The Fact Bet. The fact bet is a favorite in and around the tavern. Often it is innocent enough. Someone asks how many miles it is from wherever they are to, say, Miami. A discussion ensues and pretty soon people are taking bets on the answer.

Sometimes fact bets are more devious. One person states a dubious-sounding piece of information like "Hawaii is farther south than Florida" or "The sun is closer to the earth in winter than summer." Someone refutes him, a bet is made, and a reference book consulted. As might be expected, the unlikely fact turns out to be true.

The Sucker Bet

A sucker bet is so-called for the fact that while it appears impossible for the person who proposes it to win, it is in fact impossible for him to lose. Many people consider these wagers to be out-and-out larceny. Those with the ability to chuckle at themselves will usually not take it so seriously, at least when only a small sum of money is involved, which is usually the case. Here is a sample of the sucker line:

The bettor takes a glass of beer, declaring that he can drink the entire glass and still have enough left to another drink. If the challenge is accepted the bettor drinks down the beer, then places 50 cents in the bottom of the glass, "enough left over for another drink."

Or, the bettor tells the chump that if given a dollar he, the bettor, will be able to tell the serial number of the bill without looking. The sucker gives him a bill and the bettor rattles off some number or other. Whether or not the numbers are accurate doesn't matter. The sucker has "given him the bill" and it is now rightfully the bettor's. A bargain is a bargain, after all.

Or, the bettor takes a jigger of whiskey and fills it three-quarters to the top. He announces that he will drop ten dimes into the glass without spilling the whiskey. This one is totally legitimate. To the taker's surprise, many more than ten coins will fit into the glass before it overflows.

Or, the bettor touches the tips of his index fingers together and holds them at a point directly in the center of his chest. He challenges the strongest man in the vicinity to take hold of both wrists and, without jerking, to pull his fingers apart. Sounds incredible but the strong man will fail. Try it. As long as the pulling movement is done slowly without violent jerks the fingers can not be parted. Leverage is on the bettor's side.

Or, the bettor takes a dime and places it on top of an empty (but recently cold) bottle of beer, claiming he can make the coin flip over without touching it or moving the bottle. The secret: he makes sure his hands are warm. He clutches the bottle toward the top and the heat of his fingers will cause the gas inside the bottle to expand, forcing the coin to flip over.

Or, the wiseacre bets anyone that with a single glance he can tell how many grooves are in any long-playing record. The secret: there is only one groove on every record. It is a continuous spiral.

Or, finally, no matter how hard he tries, the bettor announces, the sucker will not be able to take his wristwatch off alone. Every time the sucker then tries, the bettor takes his own watch off along with him. The sucker can never take it off "alone."

7. Gambling to Win

For the average person, gambling is a pleasurable diversion, a chance to escape, to let off steam and maybe make money while doing it. For a small minority of gamblers gambling is not a fling, but a fanaticism, one which some psychologists believe can be as addicting as alcohol or drugs. (It is known that certain players, when forced to quit gambling, undergo the same withdrawal symptoms experienced by heroin users: chills, cold sweats, diarrhea, reactions once thought to be strictly somatic in origin.) What is it that separates such people from the rest? And why is it that most of us, the supposedly more normal ones, gamble at all?

Psychology of Gambling

The average gambler, one would suppose, is motivated by the game's more obvious allurements. The average gambler simply wants to win. He *likes* to win. He enjoys the excitement and titillation of the casino. Gambling is a social sport and he is a social-sporting animal. It's a chance for him to look good, feel good . . . and so forth.

Psychologists, at the same time, claim that the roots of the impulse go far deeper than the simple explanation above, even for the average roller. According to one school of thought, gambling is a kind of by-product of man's innate desire to control the future. Once, long ago, the paraphernalia of modern gambling—the wheel, dice, and cards—was used solely for divination. The Egyptian priest cast the bones of the antelope and turned the patterns into prophecy. Playing cards had their origin in the tarot pack, which is still used for fortune telling today. Wheels have eternally been associated with various goddesses of fortune and luck. As the centuries passed, and as religion and divination parted company, the apparatus of chance was taken over by the gamesman. But never did the apparatus lose its original meaning. It is just that today the gambler uses the ancient equipment of chance to *determine* his future rather than to divine it.

Another school of thought believes gambling to be based on sexual power drives and on unresolved childhood neuroses. The games themselves likewise feed psychological appetites. In her fascinating book *Heads I Win, Tails You Lose,* Charlotte Olmstead has developed an intriguing theory of psychoanalytical gamesmanship. Ms. Olmstead begins by showing that playing cards are rife with symbols of socio-Oedipal conflicts.

The four suits, she maintains, are based on the fundamental division of society: church, state, commerce, and peasantry. The hearts, traditionally the sign of the clergy, represent all that is benign and altruistic. Spades, once swords in the tarot pack, stand for warfare, strife, the power of the state. Diamonds, the coins of the tarot, are trade and business, the money world; while clubs, originally the peasant's staff, stand for the lower strata of society, the menial workers, the laboring force. The four suits are a microcosm of society.

Then there are the cards themselves. Notice that the face cards depict the father (king), mother (queen), and son (jack), and that these are accorded the highest rank in the pack. The family unit is the nucleus of all social relationships in western society and is therefore awarded the highest position. Within the card family, though, things are far from harmonious. Two warlike and competing males surround one passive female, for while each queen carries nothing more threatening than a flower, both jacks and kings are armed with swords, axes, clubs, signs of phallic warfare. The king of hearts, however, traditionally the most benevolent of cards, buries his sword into his head (take a look), while the other kings and jacks brandish their weapons at the world. Let the other males overtly express their sexual aggressiveness.

Do people gamble to win or to lose?
Preceding pages: Slots' hypnotic whirr and bad
payoff can fulfill the chronic gambler's
compulsion to lose. Below: Determined poker
shark is already a winner to even
compete in casino's poker tournament.

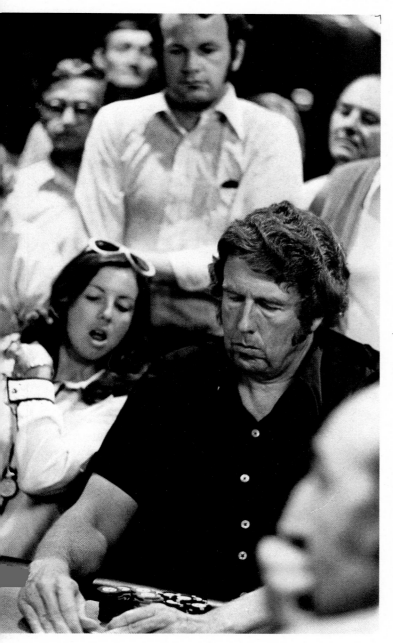

The king of hearts will suppress his own libido for the benefit of the family unit.

While kings are the patriarchs of the deck, jacks represent the younger generation. Jacks are unmarried men on the loose. They are ambitious sons whose aggressive independence threatens the father and, hence, the structure of the nuclear family. The jacks, moreover, are not always trustworthy. Two of them show only half their faces, a standard posture of duplicity. And, indeed, the very word knave has come to mean a rascal, an unprincipled person. Yet the one-eyed jacks are often afforded the highest roles as wild cards, an example of the ambivalent western attitude toward the unattached male.

Gambling games can be put to a similar analysis. In poker the better hands always show uniformity, either in suit or kind. Three 7s beat two 7s, and a flush beats both, for such is the importance we place upon conformity and peer-group gatherings. The highest hand in the game is the royal flush: the complete family is here joined by the ace, symbol of the individual ego, and by the 10, the highest of the numbered cards. Numbered cards stand for outsiders, society at large. Their worth is determined by their numerical rank. A 10 is hence a person of wealth and standing, one who is allowed to join the family's inner circle, though of course as its least ranking member. Once again the family unit is all important. And it is interesting to note that if but one card is taken away the best hand in the game becomes worthless.

A similar psychological pattern can be discerned in twenty-one. The object of this game, of course, is for the player to collect a hand which totals twenty-one or as near to this number as possible. Now significantly, the number twenty-one just happens to be the age of adulthood in western society. Could it be that those who gravitate toward this game are subconsciously striving to

Pleasures of gambling: Chips click as winnings are counted (below). Poker game provides relaxing break from daily routine (r). Elated cries of one of fifteen thousand urge favorite horse to victory (far r). Slots bring elderly woman a child's delight in hope of a jackpot (below).

gain freedom from their parents? Note that twenty-one is a game for those uncertain of their self-image. The ace, sign of the ego, is alternately the highest-ranking card in the game and the lowest, a mirror of the typical superiority-inferiority oscillations of the gambling addict. The dealer, what's more, plays a sizeable part in all of this. He is the father-mother authority figure, the person who is trying to help the player grow up and who at the same time tries to prevent it. Behind him stands an even more ominous and impersonal force, the house, representing society at large. Blackjack may thus be favored by those who have never resolved their own dominance-dependence conflicts.

Despite the fascination of such speculations, there are many psychologists who believe that the urge to gamble lies in more immediate concerns. There is, for example, narcissism, self-love. When we gamble we wish to be admired. Look how reckless I am, says the gambler, how competitive, how ingenious at picking winners. Any insightful player will admit that half the reason he enjoys the casino tables is because of the impression he makes

there on others. Role playing is thus an important motivating factor in convincing people to gamble. Casino publicity shots that show a suave gamester surrounded by worshiping females and piles of chips are not randomly conceived. They cut to the heart of the matter—the gambler's wish to be recognized and admired.

The Obsessive Gambler

Carried to excessive lengths, this indulgence at the gaming table turns into preoccupation. We arrive now at addiction, and the effort to control it through Gamblers Anonymous. The obsessive gambler traditionally is a fellow with a "big ego," with an insatiable need to be conspicuous and in the spotlight. Generally he is impatient of all criticism and has a nagging hunger for praise. Money for him is a supercharged commodity; possession of it is the ultimate testimonial to his self-image.

In his famous book, *The Psychology of Gambling,* Dr. Edmund Bergler has outlined six basic traits of the habitual gambler. Bergler was one of the first doctors to seriously study the gambler's plight, and his book is still a classic today.

According to Bergler, the first trait of the addicted gambler is habitual chance-taking. The addictive gambler thrives only when the odds are against him. His real thrill is not in winning but in meeting an impossible challenge.

Second, gambling for the addict is his paramount interest. It is his sole preoccupation. When the habitual gambler is at the track or poker table nothing else exists for him. Gambling is his sole object of attention, and everything—his social life, his friendships, his conversation—ultimately centers on that next bet.

Third, the excessive gambler is ever the optimist; and as a corollary to this, the gambler never profits from experience, no matter how dismal it may be. "Every gambler gives the impression of a man who has signed a contract with Fate," writes Bergler, "stipulating that persistence must be rewarded. With that imaginary contract in his pocket, he is beyond the reach of all logical objection and argument."

Fourth, the gambler does not stop when he is ahead. Here is what divides the addict from the nonad-

*The ubiquitous sport
of gambling attracts plungers
any time, any place, to
any game—here to slots (top)
and roulette (bottom)
in one of Tokyo's casinos.*

dict. The nonaddict knows when to quit. The addict gets himself deeper and deeper when he is winning, sometimes to the point of doubling every bet. Sooner or later he must cease to be a winner.

Fifth, the gambler eventually risks too much. Motivated by a strange self-destructive urge, the plunger finally makes the stakes too high.

Lastly, the obsessive gambler receives a tangible "pleasurable-painful" tension during the game. While most people dislike uncertainty, the gambler is excited by it. The craving for this strange sensation, Bergler observes, frequently overshadows the desire to win.

A coherent personality picture thus emerges. The obsessive gambler is a man or woman who subconsciously *wants to lose*. Whether this defeatist attitude is motivated by guilt feelings, masochism, the death wish, or something else is hard to say. The fact remains that the gambler who does not know when to stop does not want to stop until he is ruined.

Such psychological mechanisms are far from being scientific fact. No one can ultimately make total value judgments on the act of obsessive gambling, simply because each person has his own special story. Still, we must ask ourselves the question: Do people gamble because they want to win or because they want to lose? It may be difficult to answer at once; and the best proof is finally the scorecard. As we have seen throughout this book, there are smart gamblers and dumb ones. Those who drop everything at the track or casino year after year without so much as a winning week must ask themselves at some point if in fact their attitude toward winning is correct. To gamble should be to win. Common sense tells us there is really no other meaningful reason for doing it. One plays to win. Period. And if one does not win, then one had better not gamble.

Winning the Game

Gambling therefore becomes a question of formulating a winning strategy. How can a gambler best fortify himself with the will to win? Though there are as many answers to this question as there are successful gamblers, certain axioms do apply. First, there is the necessity of knowing *everything* about the game. This point cannot be stressed strongly enough. A player should understand the rules, the odds, the intricacies and tricks, or he shouldn't play. Ignorance is the number-one reason why gamblers lose.

The second important factor is realistic betting. Games such as baccarat, craps, blackjack, all have realistic wagers and sucker wagers. Anyone who stands at the crap table and fritters away his chips at hard-way bets deserves to go broke. He is a dumb gambler and dumb gamblers always lose. If a person wants to gamble seriously he must forget the slots, forget the carnival games, the keno, bingo, and rube amusements. He must go for the best-paying games and for the best bets in the best-paying games.

Third, a gambler should develop a positive attitude toward his technique, but this attitude should be tempered with common sense. It's perfectly right to believe in oneself; one would almost say that this is a prerequisite. At the same time, the type of optimism some gamblers affect, whereby their luck is forever invulnerable, is a form of madness. Believe you are going to win. But when you are losing, believe that you can also lose—at least tonight—and walk away.

Finally, learn from those who know. Read what is written on the subject of gambling and go with the advice of the wise ones. No one has ever beaten the law of averages. This is true. But some have done better at it than others, and a few have come out on top. Why not join the smart ones? You have nothing to lose.

A Few Words to the Wise from the Wise

"Limit your losses but don't limit your gains."
Gambling aphorism

"The whole key to winning is to play a conservative game and outlast the bad runs, then play more boldly and cash out ahead on a good upswing."
L. G. Holloway

"Don't buck a run. If you don't like it, lay off, but don't figure on its turning *until* it does."
L. G. Holloway

"The dice have no eyes."
Gambling aphorism

"The intelligent gambler puts a fixed limit on the amount he will bet each night, and win or lose he never exceeds that limit."
Gambling aphorism

"The best partner for dice-playing is not a just man, but a good dice-player."
Plato

"Let luck quit you; never quit your luck."
Gambling aphorism

"The only difference between a winner and a loser is character."
Nick the Greek

"Every time I enter a casino I know that at some point in the evening I will hear some player state that he 'doesn't want to win a lot—just a couple of hundred to cover expenses.'

"Isn't that terrifying?"
Nick the Greek

"Gambling: a kind of question addressed to destiny."
Theodore Reik

"The longer one plays, the bigger the chance of going broke."
Allan Wilson

"Understanding luck is as integral a part of gambling as is knowing how to cut down the odds against you."
Major A. Riddle

"Never bet more than five percent of your total capital on one bet until you are playing with house money, i.e., until you are winning."
Major A. Riddle

"There are two times in a man's life when he shouldn't speculate: when he can't afford it and when he can."
Mark Twain

"If you feel drowsy after a couple of hours [of gambling] go into the bathroom and take a look at yourself in the mirror. Tell yourself it's time to show what you're really made of.

"Then clean your fingernails.

"Wash your face and hands.

"Comb your hair, blow your nose—hell, brush your teeth if you've got a toothbrush handy! In short, go over yourself as if you're just starting the day. Make your mind a blank throughout this process. *Don't* keep thinking of the game, back there. Think of something beautiful. A sunset, perhaps, or the way the clouds hang over a mountain in the early morning. (Never of a woman; this is distracting.) And then, when you go back to the game, concentrate entirely on it once more."
Nick the Greek

"A wise player ought to accept his throws and score them, not bewail his luck."
Sophocles

"If you bet on a sure thing, be sure to save enough for carfare home."
Gambling aphorism

"There is nothing as crooked as a sucker's imagination."
Con man's aphorism

"Whenever you gamble, two considerations must be paramount because they will override all others.

First: what is your objective? Having fun, or winning, even if it's hard work?

Second: How much, i.e., how badly, do you *need* to win? How much can you afford to lose?"
Charles Goren

"There is a rhythm in the distribution of cards, a rhythm in good and bad breaks, and even a rhythm in the manner in which those breaks occur. A run of big cards is not a contradiction of this rhythm. But if dirty work is afoot, the way this run is repeated and the circumstances under which these big cards come out, hour after hour, will sound false to the finely attuned ear of a real card player."
Ely Culbertson

"The real gambler is seldom greedy. Greed is what makes a smart gambler into a stupid one."
Gambling aphorism

"I've made a study of every gambling game there is, and I stay away from the ones I can't beat. Also, I only bet the others when I think I can win."
Smart Sam, professional gambler

"Bet minimums when you're losing; bet heavy when you're winning; always make your heavy bets with the other fellow's money, not your own; quit on a losing streak, not on a winning streak."
Clement McQuaid

"Try to remember that each chip in that big pile in front of you represents a dollar. Don't let it become just a plastic chip, because tomorrow morning, sure as anything, a buck is gonna be a worth a buck again."
Tom Jones

"Make your bets at the best possible odds, and make those bets large enough to enable you to win the maximum amount."
Major A. Riddle

"Keep close track of how much money every opponent you face has lost, and make it your business to know how much he can afford to lose. The information is vital and should influence your style of play. When a player is under heavy financial pressure, and you know it, his betting can almost tell you what cards he's holding."
Nick Zographos

"One moment of lost concentration is all it takes to become a loser."
Gambling aphorism

"Never gamble if you are under the weather, emotionally upset, tired, under pressure or in a hurry. Gambling requires full psychological participation."
Robert Redoux

"Anyone who bets money on anything in the hope that luck will make him a winner is an idiot."
Pittsburgh Phil

Picture Credits

(Credits read from left to right and
from top to bottom, unless otherwise indicated)

BS   Black Star   JC   Jerry Cooke
HS   Horst Schafer   KR   Ken Regan, Camera 5
IB   Image Bank   PR   Photo Researchers

Jacket front: top: J. R. Eyerman; bottom: R. Scott Hooper.
Jacket back: R. Scott Hooper.

2-3: David Hamilton/IB; 4-5: Elliott Erwitt/Magnum, JC; 8-9:
Melchior DiGiacomo/IB; 10-11: UPI, R. Scott Hooper;
12-13: Hank de Lespinasse/IB.

Chapter 1
16-17: John Olson; 19, 20: New York Public Library; 22: R. Scott Hooper; 24-25: Inge Morath/Magnum; 26: Russell Eliot Reif/Pictorial Parade; 27: HS, Russell Eliot Reif; 28: Abigail Heyman; 30-31: UPI (all); 33: Graham Finlayson, JC, Photo Trends; 34: Herbert Eisenberg/Photo Trends, Jimmy Selkin/IB; 35: JC; 36: KR, Alexander Low, Woodfin Camp; 37: KR; 38: Richard Rowan, Jay Maisel/IB, Richard Rowan; 39: KR; R. Scott Hooper, Charles Moore/BS; 40: Bert Miller/BS (top r&l), H. Brocke, Jay Maisel/IB.

Chapter 2
46-47: Barbara Pfeffer/BS; 50: Richard Rowan; 54: Graham Finlayson/Woodfin Camp; 55: IB; 56: Christopher R. Harris; 58: J. R. Eyerman; 60-61: R. Scott Hooper (all); 62: Sue McCartney/PR; 64-65: Christopher R. Harris; 69: UPI; 70-71: Norman Snyder; 72-79: John Olson; 80-81: Norman Snyder; 83-85: Carol Bernson; 86-87: Norman Snyder; 89: KR, R. Scott Hooper; 90: KR; 91-94: R. Scott Hooper; 95: R. Scott Hooper, Farrell Grehan/IB (r); 96: Baron Wolman/Woodfin Camp (all); 98: Las Vegas News Bureau; 99: R. Scott Hooper; 100-01: Farrell Grehan/IB; 104-05: Norman Snyder; 106-07, 109: Burt Glinn/Magnum.

Chapter 3
110-11: Richard Rowan; 113: British Museum (both); 114-15: Richard Rowan; 115 (illustration): Tony Pannoni; 116: Eugene Anthony/BS; 118-19: R. Scott Hooper (all); 121: KR; 122 (all): R. Scott Hooper; 124: Ruth Adams/BS.

Chapter 4
All photographs by Norman Snyder.

Chapter 5
144-45: Melchior DiGiacomo/IB; 148-49: The Tate Gallery, London; 150-51: Yale University Art Gallery; 152: Auckland City Art Gallery; 153: Culver Pictures; 154-55: JC; 156-59: HS; 160: Leo Touchet, Magnum; 160-61: HS; 162 (top): HS/Amwest; 162 (btm)-65: HS; 166-71: JC (all); 173: UPI, HS; 175: Farrell Grehan/IB; 177: KR (top), Bert Miller/BS (l), Leo Choplin/BS (r); 178-79: H. Brocke, Melchior DiGiacomo/IB (center); 180-83: JC (all); 184: Melchior DiGiacomo/IB, Toby Rankin/IB; 186-87: UPI, Melchior DiGiacomo/IB; 188: Russell Eliot Reif; 189: Graham Finlayson/Woodfin Camp; 191: Shalmon Bernstein/Magnum.

Chapter 6
192-93: J. R. Eyerman; 195: Culver Pictures, Brown Brothers; 197: Arizona Historical Society Library (top & btm), Western History Collection/University of Oklahoma Library (center 1), Nevada Historical Society (r); 198-99: J. R. Eyerman (both); 200: Richard Rowan (top l); 200-01: Amwest; 204: Susan McCartney/PR, Bob Gelberg/PR; 206: Robert Borrow, Globe Photos; 207: JC/PR (btm 1), BS (both); 211: H. Cartier-Bresson/Magnum; 212: Amwest, Pictorial Parade, Christopher R. Harris; 214: Anne Dorkery/BS; 215: Roland Palm/BS; 217: J. R. Eyerman, KR (btm r); 218: JC; 219: KR, Richard Rowan (btm r); 220-01: KR, R. Scott Hooper (center); 222: Richard Rowan, KR; 223: J. R. Eyerman; 224: R. Scott Hooper (both); 226: Las Vegas News Bureau, R. Scott Hooper; 227: R. Scott Hooper; 228: Steve Allen/BS; 229-30 (illustration): Tony Pannoni; 231: David W. Hamilton/IB, JC/PR; 233: Melchior DiGiacomo/IB; 234, 235-36: Walter Iooss/IB; 238: Ruth Adams/BS.

Chapter 7
240-41: Bob Adelman/Magnum; 243: Christopher Springman/Camera 5, Kosti Rushman/BS, Inge Morath/Magnum; 245: HS; 246: Jean-Pierre Laffont. 250: Eugene Anthony/BS; 256: Christopher R. Harris.

Index

A

Age, in harness racing, 185–86
Allowance race, 172
Alsae (Roman dice), 112
Any craps, 119
Any seven (craps), 119
Atlantic City (New Jersey), 18,
    29, 41
Auction pinochle, 106–109

B

Baccarat, 18, 97–100,
    204, 208, 211
Backgammon, 18
Bahamas, 205
Baseball, betting on, 232–36
Basketball, betting on, 237–38
Beat the Dealer (Thorp), 57, 62
Bergler, Edmund, 245
Betting the favorite, 174
Betting the jockey, 174
Bevels, 136
Bidding (pinochle), 106–08
Big six, 225
Big 6 or 8 (craps), 120
Bingo, 18, 214–15
Blackjack, 18, 48–67, 203, 211
    advanced counting strategies of,
        59–63
    basic strategy of, 51–54
    glossary of terms for, 67
    machines, 67
    pointers for, 54–57
    principles of, 48–51.
    Silberstang System for, 65–66
    simpler counting system for, 63–65
    sucker systems for, 66

Bluff (poker), 69
Bookies, 189
Boston, 19
Bottom deal, 128
Box-number bets (craps), 120
Brag, 19
Breakage, 167
Bricks, 136
British horse racing,
    146–50

C

Call (poker), 69
Card games, 48–109
    baccarat, 97–100
    blackjack, 48–67
    faro, 100–02
    gin rummy, 102–06
    pinochle, 106–09
    poker, 68–97
Casino Gambler's Guide (Wilson),
    63
Casino gambling, 194–240
    in the Bahamas, 205
    big six, 225
    bingo, 214–15
    cheating in, 210
    chuck-a-luck, 216–25
    dealers in, 209
    deportment in, 208–09
    in Europe, 205–08
    history of, 18–23
    keno, 215–16
    in London, 203–04
    in Monte Carlo, 204–05
    in Nevada, 194–202
    private bets in, 238–39

    in Puerto Rico, 202–03
    roulette, 227–30
    slot machines, 210–14
    in sports, 232–38
    wheel of fortune, 225
Characters, glossary of,
    44–45
Cheating, 128–43
    at cards, 128–34, 137–41
    in casinos, 210
    at dice, 134–37
    in draw poker, 87–97
Chemin de fer, 97,
    208, 211
Chuck-a-luck, 18,
    20, 114, 211, 216–25
Claiming race, 172
Class and handicapping
    in harness racing, 175
    in horse racing, 164–65
Class betting system, 174
Cohen, Bernie, 24
Combination bet (lottery),
    31–32
Combination tickets,
    172
Come bet (craps), 117
Come-out (craps), 116
"Comps," 24
Compulsive gambling,
    245–47
Consistency, in harness racing,
    185
Counting strategies for blackjack
    advanced, 59–63
    Silberstang, 65–66
    simpler, 63–65

Craps, 18, 113–24, 203, 211
    dumb craps, 118–20
    odds and percentages for, 114–15,
        117–18, 123–24
    smart craps, 116–18
Craps out, 116
Cut-of-the-cards bet, 238–39

D

Daily double tickets, 172
Daubing, 139
Davis, John, 18
Dealers, 209
Dice, cheating with, 134–37
Dice games, 112–25
    craps, 113–24
    history of, 112–13
    terminology for, 125
Distance, in harness racing, 176
Dog racing, 18
Don't come bet (craps), 117
Don't pass bet (craps), 117
Doorpops, 134
Double ace (craps), 120
Double six (craps), 119
Doubling down (blackjack), 51,
    53–54
Draw poker, 20, 29, 68–70
    cheating in, 87–97
Driver strategy (harness racing),
    176
Dumb craps, 118–20
Dunes Hotel (Las Vegas), 24

E

Ecarté, 19
Eclipse, 148–50

El Casino (Bahamas), 205
Eleven (craps), 120
En-prison bets (roulette), 230
Eohippus, 146
Equalay odds, 188
Equipment, in harness racing, 185
European casino gambling, 205–08
Even-odd bet (roulette), 227–28

F

Fact bets, 239
False overhand shuffle, 134
Faro, 19, 20, 100–02, 211
Fey, Charles, 211
Field (craps), 120
Fisk, Jim 22
"Fixed limits" (poker), 68–69
Flamingo Hotel (Las Vegas), 23, 24, 195
Flats, 136
Flip-of-a-coin bet, 238
Football betting, 236–37
Forty-cent line, 232

G

Gardena (California), 29–31
General Stud Book, 150
Gin rummy, 102–06
    rules for, 102
    scoring in, 102–03
    strategy for, 103–06
Glossaries
    of blackjack terms, 67
    of dice terms, 125
    of gambling characters, 44–45
    of gambling terms, 42–44
    of horse racing, 172, 190
Good luck in threes, 174

H

Handicapping
    in harness racing, 175–86
    in horse racing, 156–65
Handicap race, 172
Hang 'em out to dry,
    176
Hard hand (blackjack),
    49, 52
Hard-way bets (craps),
    119
Harness racing, 175–86
    age and sex in, 185–86
    class in, 175
    consistency in, 185
    distance in, 176
    driver strategy in, 176
    equipment in, 185
    post position in, 176–85
    speed in, 175–76
    track size for, 185
    weight in, 176
Harolds Club (Reno),
    195–96
Hazard, 114
Heads I Win, Tails You Lose (Olmstead),
    242
Herod, 150
High-low, 29,
    70–71
High-low number bet (roulette),
    227
Hit (blackjack),
    49, 53
Hockey, 232
Holding out a card, 134
Hollywood Gin, 103

Horse racing, 146–91
   betting guidelines in, 186–89
   bookmaking and machines, 189
   glossary for, 172, 190
   handicapping in, 156–65
   harness racing, 175–86
   history of, 146–52
   parimutuel, 167
   systems for, 168–71, 174–75
   totalizator, 167–68
   touts in, 168

I

Insurance betting (blackjack),
   51, 54

J

Jackpots (poker), 69
Jai-alai, 18
Jockey and handicapping, 165
Jockey Club, 150
Junkets, 24–29

K

Keno, 215–16
King, Joe, 185
Knocking (gin rummy),
   102

L

Las Vegas, 196–202
Leaving the gate, 176
Legalization of gambling, 18
   lotteries, 31–41
   in Nevada, 194
Line bets (craps), 116–17
Loaded dice, 134

Lock grip, 134
London, 203–04
Loop the field, 176
Lotteries, 18, 31–41
Lowball, 29, 70

M

Maiden race, 172
Marked cards, 139–41
Matcher, 150
Match race, 172
Mechanics grip, 128
Melding (pinochle), 108
Melds (gin rummy), 102
Mills, Herbert Stephen, 213
Mimicking the dealer (blackjack),
   66
Missouts, 136
Monte Carlo, 204–05
Morrissey, John, 22

N

Natural (craps), 116
Nevada, 23
   casino gambling in, 194–202
"Never-bust" strategy (blackjack),
   66
New Hampshire, 41
New Orleans, 18–19
New York, 22
Numbers game, 31–41

O

Obsessive gambling, 245–47
Off-track betting, 18
Oklahoma Gin, 103
Old reliable, 174

Oller, Pierre, 167
Olmstead, Charlotte, 242
One-number bet (roulette),
   227
Optional claiming race, 172
Ortiz, Darwin, 128
Overlaid odds, 186–88

P

Pair splitting (blackjack),
   51, 54
Palming a card, 128–34
Paradise Island Casino (Bahamas),
   205
Parimutuel systems, 155, 167
Pass bet (craps), 116–17
Passers, 136
Past winners, 174
Pinochle, 106–09
   rules of, 106–08
   scoring in, 108
   strategy for, 109
Place (horse racing), 147
Place-number bets (craps), 120
Place ticket, 172
Playboy's Book of Games (Silberstang),
   65
Playing Blackjack as a Business (Revere),
   63
Point (craps), 116
Poker, 19, 68–97
   basic rules of, 68–71
   fine points of, 71–86
   in Gardena, California, 29–31
   odds in, 71–74
   spotting cheating in, 87–97
   vital statistics in, 86–87

Post position, in harness racing,
  176–85
Pot limit (poker), 69
Private bets, 238–39
Proposition bets, 51
  in craps, 119
Psychology of gambling, 242–45
Psychology of Gambling (Bergler), 245
Puerto Rico, 202–03
Punto banco, 204
Push-through, 128

Q
Quarter move, 176
Quiniela, 172

R
Races, types of, 172
Racing Form, 155, 165, 175
Raise (poker), 69
Raised-edge die, 136
Record and handicapping, 165
Red-black bet (roulette), 228
Reno (Nevada), 194
Revere, Lawrence, 63
Riffle stacking, 134
Riverboat gambling, 19
Roulette, 19, 203, 211
  in casinos, 227–30
  in European casinos, 205–208

S
San Francisco, 20
Scarne, John, 97
Scarne on Gambling, 97
Second dealing, 128
Seven-card stud poker, 70

Sex and age, in harness racing,
  185–86
Shapes, 136
Shell game, 20
Shills, 29
Shiner, 137–39
Show (horse racing), 147
Show ticket, 172
Siegel, Bugsy, 23, 195
Silberstang, Edwin, 65
Silberstang blackjack system,
  65–66
Slot machines, 210–14
Smart craps, 116–18
Smart-money playdown, 174
Smith, Raymond, 195–96
Soft hand (blackjack), 49, 52
Speed and handicapping
  in harness racing, 175–75
  in horse racing, 156
"Speed rating," 156
Sports betting, 232–38
  baseball, 232–36
  basketball, 237–38
  football, 236–37
Stake race, 172
Stay (blackjack), 49, 53
Straight bet (lottery), 31–32
Stud poker, 29, 68, 70
Sucker bets, 239
Sucker blackjack systems, 66
Sulky, 185
Super Bowl, 232

T
Table stakes (poker), 69
Ten (dice game), 114

Thorp, Edward O., 57
  blackjack advanced counting strategy
    of, 59–63
Three (craps), 120
Three-card monte, 20
Three-number bet (roulette), 228
Three wide sweep, 176
Thumb punch, 139
Totalizator, 167–68
Touts, 168
Track size, in harness racing, 185
Trotting gait, 186
Twelve-number column bet (roulette),
  228
Twenty-cent line, 232
Two-number bet (roulette), 227

U
Underlay odds, 186–88

V
Vingt-et-un, 19, 20

W
Weight and handicapping
  in harness racing, 176
  in horse racing, 164
Weintraub, Julie, 24
Wheel of fortune, 211, 225
Whist, 19
Widow (pinochle), 108
Wilson, Allan, 63
Win (horse racing), 147
Winning, 242–47
  compulsive gambling and, 245–47
  psychology of gambling and, 242–45
Win ticket, 172